WORKING UP
to PROJECT MANAGEMENT

 # *Also Available from Dorset House Publishing*

WORKING UP *to* PROJECT MANAGEMENT

HOW CRUSHING ROCKS AT THE ASPHALT PLANT PREPARED ME FOR GOVERNMENT WORK

Dwayne Phillips

DORSET HOUSE PUBLISHING
353 WEST 12TH STREET
NEW YORK, NEW YORK 10014

12 11 10 9 8 7 6 5 4 3 2 1

Dedication

*In memory of my dad, Neal Phillips,
who provided me with a job crushing rocks
and gave me an education for life.*

Acknowledgments

Acting on the conviction that some things are better said late than never, I offer heart-felt thanks to all those people who helped me through my four years working part-time at Louisiana Paving Company. Thanks in particular to Ray, Jackson, Mr. and Mrs. Brister, Greene, P-John, and many others whose faces and lessons I can remember, but whose names escape me.

A special thanks to my father, Neal Phillips, who landed the job at the asphalt plant for me and taught me more there and elsewhere than anyone else I have ever known.

Thanks go as well to Lynn Hill, Robert Johnson, and Johanna Rothman, each of whom read the draft manuscript and provided invaluable feedback; and to the editors at Dorset House, for their willingness to take a chance on this writer's ruminations. As I met these and other fine people at some of Jerry Weinberg's Amplifying Your Effectiveness Conferences and writers' workshops, it is to Jerry that I owe the piper's song. Appreciations to all.

Contents

Introduction..**XV**

THE WORK XVI

THE EXPERIENCE XVII

THE MEMORIES XVIII

THE LESSONS XVIII

Chapter One: Tools...**3**

THE FLAT-POINT SHOVEL 4

PROJECT PROCESS AND CULTURE BASICS 5

WORK ENVIRONMENTS AND TOOLS 7

UNDERSTANDING WORK ENVIRONMENTS 8

MATCHING TOOLS TO ENVIRONMENTS 10

USING THE RIGHT TOOL 11

    Thoughts on the Flat-Point Shovel 12

THE CHEATER PIPE 13

SIMPLE TOOLS CAN MULTIPLY EFFECTIVENESS 14

THERE'S PROJECT-MANAGEMENT MAGIC 15

IN LITTLE SCRAPS OF PAPER

LEARNING THROUGH EXPERIENCE 17

A CHANGE TOOL 18

    Thoughts on the Cheater Pipe 19

THE HARD HAT 20

INFRASTRUCTURE AS A TOOL 21

CHANGING PERSPECTIVES 24

TOOLS? WHAT TOOLS? MAKING TOOLS VISIBLE 26

    Thoughts on the Hard Hat 28

CONCLUSIONS 29

REFERENCES 30

Chapter Two: Raw Materials 31

COOKING WITH ROCKS 32

EMPTY BOXES 34

EXTRA PEOPLE 35

GROWING PEOPLE 36

LOOKING FOR HOT ROCKS 37

USING HOT ROCKS 37

Thoughts on Cooking With Rocks 40

THE BUCK FOLDING KNIFE 40

EXPECTATIONS 42

DIVERSITY AND CONFORMITY 43

OPEN EYES 45

Thoughts on the Buck Folding Knife 46

MAKING WRENCHES 46

"GOOD ENOUGH" TOOLS 48

MR. PRACTICAL 50

"WASTE NOT, WANT NOT" IS NEVER ANY FUN 51

FINDING WHAT'S IMPORTANT 52

Thoughts on Making Wrenches 54

CONCLUSIONS 55

REFERENCES 55

Chapter Three: Integrity 56

WORKING WITH MY DAD 57

WITNESSING INTEGRITY 58

MANAGING WITH MULTIPLE VIEWS 60

HONORING PEOPLE 62

PRACTICING INTEGRITY 63

Thoughts on Working With My Dad 65

FLAGGING TRAFFIC 65

THE LEAST WAS THE MOST 67

THE INTEGRITY FLAG 67

IT'S ALL ABOUT PEOPLE 69

STAND STILL AND OBSERVE 69

USING YOUR SENSES 71

STANDING STILL WHILE I CHANGE 73

Thoughts on Flagging Traffic 75

WORDS IN BOOKS 76

FEAR AND RESPECT—AND CHOICE 77

WORKING WITH AND THROUGH PEOPLE 78

FEAR AT WORK ...79
RESPECT AT WORK ...79
CHOICE AT WORK ...80
WORKING WITH ADULTS ...81
DIVERSITY ...81
FEAR NO EVIL ...84
BACK TO ADULTS ...87
Thoughts on Words ...88
CONCLUSIONS ...89
REFERENCES ...90

Chapter Four: Language ...**91**
THE HOSE-PIPE ...92
A MODEL OF COMMUNICATION ...94
FILTERS ...96
THAT'S SHOW BUSINESS ...98
A ROSE BY ANY OTHER NAME WOULD SMELL AS SWEET ...99
Thoughts on the Hose-Pipe ...101
SIGNING WITH AN X ...101
SOME THINGS THAT CANNOT STILL EXIST DO STILL EXIST ...103
ASSUMING AND FORGETTING ...104
FEARING, FORGETTING, AND ASSUMING ...105
FINDING THE DINOSAURS ...107
RIDING THE DINOSAURS ...108
Thoughts on Signing a Name ...110
CONCLUSIONS ...110
REFERENCES ...111

Chapter Five: Culture ...**112**
SANDWICH SURPRISES ...112
HONG KONG ...114
NIGERIA ...115
PAKISTAN ...117
SEEING THE WORLD ON A DOLLAR A DAY ...118
TRAVELING LESS THAN A MILE ...119
TRAVEL TO THE LAND OF TINTED HAIR AND SHINY STUDS ...120
TRAVELING IN TIME ...121
Thoughts on Sandwiches ...122
TWO SETS OF RULES ...122
MY ADVICE ...124
TAKE MY ADVICE, PLEASE ...125
TAKE MY ADVICE, SAY I TO MYSELF ...127

ADVICE FOR MY ADVICE 129
CONCLUSIONS 130
REFERENCES 131

Chapter Six: Risk and Opportunity 132

BENDING METAL 133
RISKY BUSINESS 134
HALF EMPTY OR HALF FULL? 137
CHANCE—AND—RISK AT WORK 138
BEING READY FOR GOOD OUTCOMES 141
    Thoughts on Bending Metal 142
HOLDING ONTO CHAINS 143
FACING RISK 144
SOME THINGS ARE TOUGH 145
SOME PEOPLE AREN'T SO TOUGH 146
RISK MANAGEMENT 148
    Identify 148
    Plan 150
    Set Triggers 150
    Observe 151
    Act 151
    Thoughts on Holding Onto Chains 152
CONCLUSIONS 153
REFERENCES 154

Chapter Seven: Practice 155

OPERATING THE FRONT-END LOADER 157
SOME THINGS TAKE TIME 158
MOST PEOPLE TAKE TIME 160
EVERYONE KNOWS THAT! 161
WORKING WITH LEARNERS 161
    The Trade-School Model 161
    The Liberal-Arts Model 162
CHOOSING A MODEL 163
    Thoughts on the Front-End Loader 165
PAINTING BLACK AND YELLOW STRIPES 166
ONE STEP AT A TIME 167
    Thoughts on One Step at a Time 169
IGNORING THE STRIPES 169
ADULT WORK 171
PAINTING BEGINS WITH A "P" 172
    Plan 172

Persevere 173
Perform 173
A Pat on the Back 174
Thoughts on Painting Black and Yellow Stripes 175
WET ROCKS AND HOT DAYS 176
THIS IS *NOT* WHAT THEY TOLD ME! 177
BEING PREPARED 179
BELIEVE REALITY 181
Thoughts on Wet Rocks and Hot Days 182
THE ROAD CREW'S LUNCH BREAK 183
IT WAS MY TURN 184
BILLBOARDS 187
GUERRILLAS 189
CLOSING THE GAP 190
Training 190
BILLBOARDS ON MY DESK 191
Thoughts on the Road Crew's Lunch Break 192
CONCLUSIONS 193
REFERENCES 193

Introduction

I used to crush rocks in Louisiana. That's how I paid for college. I was a laborer for the Louisiana Paving Company, and between December of 1976 and May of 1980, I worked crushing rocks part-time at LPC's asphalt plant. If I recall correctly, I was paid $4.15 an hour, a rate that I don't think changed even once in four years.

Louisiana is hot for most of the year (at least 95° Fahrenheit during the summer), and when I worked at the asphalt plant, the place felt like someone had put a dozen heaters in a steamroom. Whatever the season, an asphalt plant is an uncomfortable place, especially so when it's in Louisiana, and the constant mixing and moving around of materials—rocks, sand, and dirt—in and out of dump trucks, front-end loaders, and bulldozers makes plenty of noise. Fine particles of crushed rock and rock dust coat everything. The mixing, heating, and transporting of materials kicks dust up into the air, and then it floats back down and covers everything all over again. The dust is so fine that drops of water bead up on it instead of soaking in.

The asphalt plant is where the black material used to pave most roads is mixed and made. The plant itself is a structure made of a mass of steel machinery the size of several houses strung together in a row. The machinery jumbles two sizes of rock with sand and dirt, heats the mixture to 400° F, mixes in pure asphalt (a liquid petroleum product), and drops the scalding concoction into dump trucks for delivery to a road-building site.

Laborers at the asphalt plant did just what the job title implies: They labor at every little, bothersome, and unskilled job that happened along, including picking up trash, shoveling materials, finding parts, running errands, and, of course, crushing rocks. I did that job for those four years, working between semesters at college and during summer breaks.

THE WORK

Asphalt is made from two different but uniform sizes of rock, and my primary task at the plant was to crush rocks to reduce them to the required size. The large ones needed to be about the size of a nickel; the small ones, about one quarter of the size of a dime. Sometimes, the raw materials that came to the plant were too big for either. When that happened, I had to crush rocks.

I am thankful that I wasn't expected to do this job with a sledgehammer as a tool. We used a machine with two large steel wheels that turned slowly. The wheels—like the ones on an oversized steamroller—were about six feet in diameter and six-feet long, with their axles positioned parallel to one another at a distance from each other equal to the diameter of the size of rocks we wanted. Using a conveyor-belt system, we fed rocks between the wheels so that the rocks would get crushed between the wheels and then fall onto another conveyor system that carried them away.

To you, this may all sound nice and neat and easy, but you probably won't think so after I describe the full process: Working in extreme heat and dust, the operator of a front-end loader would dump scoopfuls of uncrushed rocks into a large bin that slowly funneled rocks onto the conveyor system that carried them to be crushed between the steel wheels. Once crushed, the rocks spilled out onto the next conveyor system, which carried them away, and then dropped them onto a pile where the same front-end-loader operator would have his vehicle positioned to scoop up the crushed rocks to transport them to another area on the Louisiana Paving Company's grounds.

The job of crushing rocks, like most other jobs at the asphalt plant, was not nice and neat and easy. Uncrushed rocks inevitably spilled out of the bin and off the first conveyor belt; crushed rocks spilled off the next belt before getting to the spot where they were to drop onto the pile to be scooped up by the front-end loader, bouncing everywhere they weren't supposed to be. Multiple piles of rocks grew steadily, eventually threatening to clog the machinery unless someone kept them from accumulating. Because the errant rocks formed piles that usually were too close to the machinery's steel wheels and conveyor-belt system, the front-end-loader could not be used to remove them.

The job had to be done manually by a laborer with a shovel—a laborer like me. I would walk around the rock crusher with my shovel, scoop up the spilled rocks, and throw them onto one large pile that the front-end-loader operator could get his equipment to for removal. Rather than nice and neat and easy, my job was hot and dirty and backbreaking, but it was an experience that I can now appreciate better in the context of project management.

THE EXPERIENCE

Rocks *are* heavy and dirty. Shoveling rocks is hot, dirty, and back-straining work. What was best about my experience at the asphalt plant came from being around the people who worked there. I was the college kid, and people knew I was there between semesters. They understood that when I would one day graduate, I most likely would take a different path in life.

A few of the men had graduated from college, and they now worked as company supervisors. About half of the men had graduated from high school and held skilled jobs as equipment operators and mechanics. The remainder of the men had little schooling, and some could neither read nor write. Trained to operate simple equipment and to work as laborers like myself, many of these men were blacks and had grown up in rural, segregated Louisiana and Mississippi. The school of hard knocks was their alma mater. These men were trained to do things by the book, but most knew when to throw away the book and go off on their own. It was from these men that I learned the most about how to work and how to manage.

Viewing my time at the plant as a temporary crossing, all of the men treated me with more respect than I was due, teaching me valuable lessons about the importance of the right tools, raw materials, integrity, language, culture, risk and opportunity, and practice—lessons I would eventually put to use in my chosen career and which now have become the foundation for this book.

THE MEMORIES

My experiences at the asphalt plant had faded into the recesses of my memory until the summer of 2001 when the management company that operates the office building I work in excavated the parking lot and built a three-level parking garage, right outside my second-floor office window. My colleagues and I—a group of engineers who mostly build things on paper and PowerPoint—would stand at the window like small boys and watch with envy as workers built the parking garage from concrete and steel.

I was employed as a project manager during that summer of 2001, but seeing the clothing the construction workers wore, and watching their mannerisms and the techniques they used to do their job, I felt transported back in time to my years at the asphalt plant. Sitting back at my desk and attending to project management duties while I remembered my days at the plant, I slowly realized that many of the things I had done some twenty years earlier taught me much of what I know about project management. There is a relationship between crushing rocks and applying tools and technologies to create twenty-first-century systems.

During that summer, I kept a pad of paper and a pencil on my desk and jotted a note whenever something in the garage construction project triggered another memory of the asphalt plant. Slowly, my notes accumulated, filling many sheets of that pad of paper.

A year or so later, I realized that I had collected enough tips and techniques to think about developing them into a book. I hope that reading what developed will bring you as much enjoyment and learning as writing it brought me.

THE LESSONS

I did not always like my job at the asphalt plant. I was young and had dreams for the future. The asphalt plant was not in these dreams. I couldn't wait to graduate from college and leave the plant for good. That was foolish of me.

In retrospect, I believe that working at the plant taught me as much about projects and management as did pursuing an engineering degree. It certainly prepared me better for my career in project management.

I apologize in advance to anyone who reads this book and knows much about asphalt plants. My stint at the plant happened a long time ago, and there were many things about the workings of the plant that I probably never understood. If readers see that my description of how an asphalt plant is built and works is wrong, please correct me. In this book, I attempt to pass along life-lessons I learned from working at the asphalt plant. If you remember little else from this book, I hope it will be the following chief lessons:

1. *I can learn something anywhere.*
2. *I can learn something from anyone.*

I hope these remain true for me, for the remainder of my life, and I hope you can apply them as well.

August 2007   —D.P.
Reston, Virginia

WORKING UP
to PROJECT MANAGEMENT

ONE

Tools

Tools are things I use. I intend the word "things" to be as vague a definition of tools as possible. Writers aren't supposed to be vague, but being specific with the subject of tools limits thinking.

While I was a laborer for the Louisiana Paving Company working at the asphalt plant, I learned how to think of tools in different ways. Thinking about tools has increased effectiveness at work—both for my coworkers and for myself.

The tools I used at the asphalt plant were physical tools that I manipulated with my hands. The other laborers and I used these tools in the expected ways, but we also used them in unexpected and creative ways. The tools allowed us to do our work.

When I graduated from college in 1980, I left the asphalt plant and entered the world of engineering, and then, eventually, the world of engineering management. While I sometimes am still able to work outdoors at field sites, most of my professional work these days is performed in the office. I do a lot of talking in meetings and at conferences, and I read a lot of documents. The tools I used at the asphalt plant have disappeared from my daily life. I no longer have much need for shovels, levers, wedges, pulleys, or screws. Thinking about the tools I used back then and the tools I use now got me to thinking about how people accomplish "work."

Wondering about parallels between then and now, I started to look more closely at the tools I use in the office, to see how my years as a rock-crusher prepared me for my white-collar life. I learned to notice what instruments and techniques we use in the office and in meetings. By identifying patterns of use associated with the tools, I am better able to pick and choose among them.

Back at the asphalt plant, we used tools in varied and creative ways. It occurred to me that if I could experiment with office tools as I had with those at the asphalt plant, perhaps I could put more tools to good use.

That was my thinking. This chapter relates part of my journey with tools, linking ones I used in Louisiana with ones I use today as an engineer and manager. As you read, I hope you will notice tools available to you and see how they affect your work and that of the people who work with you. I also hope you will experiment with new ways to use old tools.

THE FLAT-POINT SHOVEL

At the asphalt plant, the flat-point shovel was the laborer's fundamental tool. This shovel was essential to my job because of the way the asphalt plant itself was structured. The area under the actual plant machinery was smooth, hard cement, but other areas—the area under the rock crusher, for example—weren't cement. Those areas had a rock base that had compacted to form a smooth, hard surface of particles of crushed rocks, dust, and sand.

Rocks, dirt, and sand—we called the mix "materials"—grew rapidly into piles of all shapes and sizes around the plant machinery. As described in the Introduction, this happened because materials were moved about by a system of conveyor belts that were positioned at different levels and at right angles to each other—a system that seemed precise and well engineered, but wasn't. A conveyer belt would transport materials in one direction and dump them onto a lower-level belt that would move them in a different direction, carrying them away at a 90-degree angle from the first conveyor. At the junctions, materials would spill messily across the second belt's surface, building up in piles or tumbling and ricocheting off the belt to the hard area below.

Every few hours, another laborer or I would remove the piles of materials from the conveyer belts so that a front-end loader could take them away. Feet planted squarely on the ground, I had to grab my shovel, scoop the materials from beneath the moving belt and throw shovelfuls onto any of the new piles we'd make off to the side of the belt area. The asphalt-plant machinery continued to operate during this clean-up, spewing dust everywhere, covering and choking me and the other laborers with particulate and grit.

The flat-point shovel was the perfect tool for the job, and each laborer had one. I never went anywhere on the plant grounds without that shovel. It enabled me to scrape clean an area of rock-littered surface, slide the shovel under the materials, and scoop a full load with each try. There was no wasted effort, motion, or time.

For whatever reasons, flat-point shovels fascinated me back then, probably because people away from the asphalt plant didn't use them. Where I lived—in a rural, dairy-farming area in Tangipahoa Parish in Louisiana—country folk used shovels to dig holes and ditches and to work gardens. Shovels were common, but they were never flat-point shovels. In Tangipahoa Parish, people used round-point or sharp-point shovels, which were easy to plunge into the ground to make a hole. A flat-point shovel wasn't any good for that type of work—the flat-ended blade wouldn't puncture the surface.

From seeing people work with different types of shovels, I learned a lesson about utility. The flat-point shovel was great at the asphalt plant, but it was not useful on a rural farm. The round- and sharp-point shovels were practical on the farm, but they were all but useless at the plant. Debating which shovel type was superior was foolish. Clearly, the tools themselves did not change, but how useful each was depended on the setting. The lesson:

When the environment is changed, the tool may need to be changed.

PROJECT PROCESS AND CULTURE BASICS

I went to work for the United States government soon after I left the asphalt plant and had graduated from college. As most of my career has been spent working on engineering and technical projects in various sections of the Department of Defense, I've become accustomed to the government's way of conducting such projects, usually by contracting with nongovernment entities to build or maintain software and systems the government ultimately will acquire.

Stated in the most basic terms, here's the way things work: The contractor designs the system, builds it, tests it, delivers it, and often operates it after delivery. Prior to award of a contract, however, analysts for the government prepare documents specifying what system or software the government wants built, and submits these documents for bid. Bidding contractors prepare proposals to convince the government that they can build the correct system at a good price.

Relying on contractors to build and maintain their software systems requires considerable *oversight*, with someone from the specific department of government assigned to monitor the contractor's progress. Typically, that person visits the contractor monthly to review progress. Each month, the contractor presents a summary of what it has accomplished since the previous meeting, covering topics such as its adherence to the agreed-upon schedule and budget, and providing a status report on the system's performance to date. At the end of each session, the government representative returns to the office and reports to his or her management on the contractor's progress and status, particularly in terms of schedule, cost, and performance. Adding a level of control over the project, upper-level managers within the government monitor how well the representative is overseeing the contractor.

Government acquisition also involves a battery of *formal reviews*. Generally, the contract begins with a meeting at which managers from both the government and the contractor discuss the project and verify that they agree on what is to be built and how it is to be built. At key points during the project, the contractor hosts other formal reviews, the goal of which is to ensure that the contractor is on track before embarking on a new phase. For example, before beginning design, the contractor may host a review to show that it fully understands the requirements of the system. Before starting to build the system, the contractor may hold a review to demonstrate that it has a complete and accurate design upon which to build the system according to formal specifications.

Oversight, formal reviews, and *documentation* are part and parcel to government projects because such projects use public funds and ultimately are accountable to taxpayers. If a project consumes money and does not produce a system, the demand for accountability can be especially stringent.

As I learned ways to design and deliver systems according to government spec, I came across a tool to use to improve my productivity: process models, the best known of which is the Capability Maturity Model Integrated (CMMI) created by the Software Engineering Institute (SEI) of Carnegie-Mellon in Pittsburgh, Pennsylvania. The U.S. Department of Defense funds the SEI, so it is no surprise that the CMMI follows the government-mandated pattern of oversight, formal reviews, and documentation, as does the process tool advocated in the ISO-9000 series.

Back then, as now, not everyone favored the government's long-drawn-out process of oversight, formal reviews, and documentation, at the end of which would come delivery of the system. Critics argue that such practice adds large amounts of time and cost to a project and little value.

From advocates of evolutionary and iterative deliveries of a system, I learned new tools and the value of bringing a product quickly to market—the key to an entity's ability to outlast the competition and survive in the marketplace. Microsoft stands out as a prime example of a company that is dedicated to delivering product quickly, even when defects are known to exist in the product. Microsoft understands that consumers will tolerate some defects, for some period of time, if they have a product in hand.

Learning how best to use these seemingly opposite approaches was facilitated by my memory of that long-ago debate about flat-point versus round-point shovels. The best tool is the one that suits the environment, the setting, and the use to which the tool—or the process, or the method—will be put. The basic government process is suited to the government and its environment of spending and accounting for public funds. The quick-to-market process is suited to private business and its environment of right-now demand for goods.

WORK ENVIRONMENTS AND TOOLS

The lesson about work environments and tools can apply to many fields of endeavor. Obviously, the asphalt plant and the rural home provide different environments; equally obvious is the fact that flat-point shovels and round-point shovels are different tools. What may not be so obvious are the differences between other work environments and tools.

UNDERSTANDING WORK ENVIRONMENTS

By comparing two work environments, I can discover whether they are different and, if they are, how they are different. Determining how they are different—in terms of people, process, and product—helps me understand whether the tools that succeed in one work environment can succeed in another.

People are key to the workplace environment. They can be described in terms of, say, salary, experience, ability, and even in terms of something as arbitrary as their rate of turnover. Differences between people play a large role in what types of tools will be warranted: For example, tools that reduce the time required to perform mundane and repetitive tasks make great sense for people who earn high salaries; for people being paid low salaries, time-saving tools that cost a lot of money are not a wise investment.

Another effective way to estimate what the success of specific tools will be in any given work environment is to examine differences between the abilities of the people doing the work. Ability—how each person's education, experience, and skills mesh with the demands of the job—is a good indicator of success. Thinking back to my job at the asphalt plant, I remember that it only took me a couple of minutes to acquire the knowledge needed to operate the front-end loader, but it was weeks before I had the experience and skill I needed to use the equipment even marginally well.

Process in a workplace also can be used to predict the likelihood of success that specific tools will have in a specific environment. Each place I have worked has had an accepted process that workers follow to do their job (although most places did not document the process). Over the years, I came to realize that some of the factors that can both affect and help describe process or culture—the way a particular organization always performs tasks—include physical location, size, and how formal an organization is.

Although cultures may vary from one region of a country to another and between different countries throughout the world, it is somewhat possible to generalize about culture and process in, say, same-size organizations by region. For example, because the climate in much of California is temperate year-round, the work culture does not change much from month to month throughout the year. In contrast, the culture of a company situated in northern New York State, where summer days are long and mild and winter days are short and harsh, will change markedly as people behave and work differently during the different seasons. From this generalized knowledge, one can safely choose tools that have a likelihood of success.

As noted above, process is affected by the size of an organization. Large organizations require a more formal structure in order to function at their best, and their managers tend to set up working groups or interface committees (teams with designated chairpersons and appointed record-keepers) because these help dispersed groups to coordinate their efforts. Small organizations are more nimble and can get business done with only a few people getting together to work through issues. A white board is a handy tool for a small organization, but it would not provide an adequate or permanent record for a large one.

The third factor I look at when assessing a work environment is *product*. Product can be divided into tangible goods and services. Organizations that provide services generally have a culture that is different from organizations that provide tangible goods. In addition, the culture in organizations that produce disposable goods generally differs from that of workplaces that produce durable goods that are built to last. It is understood that some products are designed to last a lifetime while others are meant to be replaced every few years.

Take the automotive industry, for example, which has had to shift to manufacturing more durable product because many customers in the United States now keep cars an average of six to ten years instead of trading in a vehicle every two to four years, as was common practice a generation ago. Built-in quality makes the automotive product more valuable.

Other work environments survive by selling service. Customers pay more for food at a restaurant than at the grocery store because it is prepared for them according to their preference and then served to them, hopefully with a smile.

MATCHING TOOLS TO ENVIRONMENTS

What constitutes a tool is not always obvious. Sometimes, the hardest task in matching tools to environments is first seeing what is—or is not—a tool and then seeing *everything* the tool can be used to do. By looking at specific tools in the context of the people, process, and product framework, I find that I can more easily determine how and where to use each tool.

People in a work environment, of course, are "tools." Although people are not the kind of tools that may be used and then cast aside, they are tools in the sense that they are "used" to get work done. As an employer of people on projects, I want to provide training, opportunities for rewarding experiences, and salaries that are commensurate with industry standards as well as with the job they've done. I also want to leave them with the mental and emotional well-being they'll need to tackle another project. The descriptors of people discussed earlier (salary, experience, ability, and rate of turnover) are useful in deciding how to match people to environments.

Process also can be viewed as a tool that can be matched with environment. Although usually thought of as a component of environment, process can be a most useful tool. By understanding an organization's process, I can use it to accomplish work. For example, in groups that are organized in the classic hierarchy—with the chief at the top, several people under the authority of the chief, and similar groups under them—I can use the stable structure of the integrated group to accomplish work. In the type of organization prevalent in the movie industry, where people come together to make a movie but go in different directions once the work is done, I can use fluidity as a tool.

Products such as computers, telephones, copy machines, and fax machines clearly are tools used in most offices and in many homes, but white boards, walls covered with five-inch by seven-inch cards and yarn, and rolls of butcher's paper are perfect tools for some environments.

Matching the right tools to the environment and seeing the essence of an environment to which to match proper tools requires common sense and some analysis, but it is not rocket science. By looking at work in terms of people, process, and product, the match between tool and environment can be a satisfying and successful one.

USING THE RIGHT TOOL

The challenge that the flat-point versus round-point shovel lesson presents parallels what managers must do when matching tools to the environment. In order to match the right tools to the environment, managers must observe and they must question.

By *observing*, I mean using the five senses to examine the environment and the tools. To some people, observing may only involve what they see with their eyes. However, I define "observing" to include all sensing that comes with touching, listening, smelling, tasting, and seeing. Sensing also involves the emotions I feel and the reactions I have. Touching, listening, smelling, tasting, and seeing things at an asphalt plant is vastly different from what I observe and feel when I am on a rural, dairy farm. Observing the differences between an engineering office in the Pentagon and a law office in New Orleans should also involve these five senses.

Seeing something that is unfamiliar often helps me notice the particulars of something that is familiar. Working at the asphalt plant and seeing its smooth, hard surfaces helped me to notice the softness of the soil around my home. As a manager, I try to observe the environment at other organizations in order to identify tools I may want to use there that would not be practical in my own environment.

After observing for a while, I begin *questioning*. I don't wait until I've finished observing before asking questions because the job of observing never ends. Asking questions and listening to the answers tells me whether I am using the best tools for the environment. The first question I ask is, *"Can tools from this environment be useful for my organization?"*

If environments are different, the same tools may or may not be applicable. Organizations can be different in many respects, but if they are alike in one attribute, the same tools may work in both environments. For example, although the government environment is different from the dot-coms, both can use word processors. Government employees and their dot-com counterparts may not use word processors in the same manner, but both can use them to good effect.

Next, I ask questions having to do with environmental change. Most environments change with time, sometimes because of deliberate decisions and sometimes because of external influences, but regardless of the reason, when change occurs, the tools may need to change with them.

The concept of changing tools when the environment changes leads to the next question, *"When will I need to adopt tools like those used in this other environment?"*

When the day comes (if ever) that my mother in Tangipahoa Parish decides to install a smooth, hard, blacktop driveway, I'll recommend that she buy a flat-point shovel to scrape it clean. When my government office starts developing large amounts of custom software, I'll recommend that we install high-capacity data networks so we can outsource work to India and be able to communicate with our outsourcers continuously and without time delays. By observing and questioning how things differ in other environments and noting what tools work best there, I'll know to change these things. If I let my tools lag behind changes to my environment, my organization may not survive the change.

Any change of tools means that I must go back to observing. The knowledge that the observe-and-question steps form a cycle that never ends is proof-positive that I work in a dynamic setting that never grows stale and in which I will never be bored. That's decidedly good news!

Thoughts on the Flat-Point Shovel

For some years, I was exceedingly handy with a flat-point shovel. I could scoop and throw rocks and sand as well as anyone. The feel and sound of that shovel scraping across a concrete base belonged to me. Ten years or so after leaving the asphalt plant, I had occasion to pick up that shovel again to scrape sand from a concrete strip where a security gate was to roll across an opening. Someone standing nearby remarked that it appeared I had handled such a shovel before. Ten years of neckties and meetings had not erased the rhythm of using the flat-point shovel from me.

Just as my shovel worked well at the plant but was lousy in the home garden, many iterative and evolutionary delivery ideas that people rave about in private industry cause years of frustration when tried out in government. The tools that work so well in one environment don't always fit another, but managers should keep on observing and questioning until one day they may.

THE CHEATER PIPE

I'm convinced that an asphalt plant would deteriorate and collapse into a corroded pile of steel, nuts, bolts, and grit-encrusted parts in a month if the plant went that long without maintenance. The vibration, heat, and corrosive materials wear on the steel of the plant. In Louisiana, add in the humidity and rain to quicken the decay.

Maintenance work had to be performed at the Louisiana Paving Company several times a month, much of it done with a cheater pipe to loosen the large and badly corroded nuts and bolts holding the plant together.

A cheater pipe fits over the handle end of a wrench and increases the length and turning power of the wrench. The cheater pipes we used at the asphalt plant ran anywhere from six- to ten-feet long, making our souped-up wrenches a bit longer than six- to ten-feet long. Because torque equals the force applied to the end of the wrench handle multiplied by the length of the handle, using a six-foot handle instead of a six-inch handle makes quite a difference.

Two-person teams worked the cheater pipe/wrench devices at the plant: One person held the wrench tightly on the stuck bolt while the other person walked the end of the cheater pipe through a big arc. Once the bolt loosened, this procedure turned it a quarter turn, with the process repeated until the bolt was loose enough to turn with only the wrench itself. Being a part-timer and the youngest person on the job, I always had the assignment of placing the wrench on the bolt and holding it in place while someone else walked the arc with the cheater piper.

This sounds fairly straightforward, but once again, theory and reality did not match at the asphalt plant. My job was considerably worse than it would seem because the stuck bolts were usually on the underside of machinery. I had to crawl and wiggle my way through the dust or mud under the equipment, lie on my back, and hold the wrench firmly in place above my head. While the corroded bolt turned slowly, the metal bits of corrosion would fall from the bolt down onto my waiting face. There is nothing quite like the feeling of corroded metal glued by perspiration to one's face.

In addition to learning to keep my eyes and mouth shut while performing this task, I learned the lesson of the cheater pipe:

The simplest things can multiply effectiveness.

SIMPLE TOOLS CAN MULTIPLY EFFECTIVENESS

A cheater pipe is just a simple pipe, and there are few things as simple as a pipe. I don't think anyone at the plant ever went to a supplier and bought a pipe to be used as a cheater pipe. We just used pieces of scrap pipe left over from other jobs. Nevertheless, the cheater pipe was invaluable because it multiplied our effectiveness, enabling us to turn bolts that we would not otherwise have been able to turn.

The effect of torque is impressive. The cheater pipe turned a strong man and a weak (I'll admit it!) college kid into a force with the strength of Hercules. A six-foot cheater pipe is twelve times longer than a six-inch handle on a wrench. Adding a cheater pipe of that length to the wrench handle gives one man walking the arc the strength equivalent to twelve men trying to use a wrench with a six-inch handle.

There have been times during my career when I tried to take a complex approach to solving a problem, failed miserably, regrouped, and saw a simple approach that worked. Each time, the failure forced me to rethink the problem from a different angle and helped me identify the true nature of the problem. Once I saw that, I invariably have come up with a simpler solution. All those encounters with the cheater pipe taught me that the simple solution is often the best approach to take.

THERE'S PROJECT-MANAGEMENT MAGIC IN LITTLE SCRAPS OF PAPER

One task I have performed time and time again throughout my career is project planning. I have helped plan projects that required only two people working for two weeks on up to projects staffed with eighty people working overtime for the better part of five years. In the mid-1980s, I began using project-management software that ran on PCs. I read through the manuals, experimented, and planned projects using these tools. Over the next few years, I fell in love with what these tools could do.

Whenever I needed to plan a project, I sat down at my PC and opened up my handy project-management program *du jour*. The size of the project never daunted me, for I had at my fingertips what was clearly the world's greatest tool. I'd spend the first hours entering background information, happy with the knowledge that the tool could be used to manipulate the information later on as I talked through the details of the project with my coworkers and staff. Eager to make use of this great device, I would ask people for their opinions and input on the project plan, which I then would enter into the tool. People sat quietly by as I deftly maneuvered through the input screens, oblivious to their twiddling thumbs and increasingly exchanged glances.

As time went on, I asked coworkers and staff more questions about the project. Most of their answers were correct, but when I suspected that my people were "mistaken" in their ideas about projects, I adjusted their answers and entered "corrected" information.

When the results produced by each of these efforts were embarrassingly poor and the project plans laughable, I decided the reason for failure was that my people didn't understand the details of projects like I did. *If only they had studied the complexities of these marvelous tools like I had, we could plan projects that would succeed,* or so I thought to myself.

I came to my senses in the early 1990s when I learned of another project-planning tool. This one wasn't complex to learn or costly to purchase. All that was required was a packet or two of five-inch by seven-inch index cards and some string, masking tape, colored markers, and a blank wall. With these simple items at hand, groups of people could participate in project planning. Whenever a person thought of a task needed in a project, he or she wrote that task on an index card and taped it to the wall. When there were enough cards on the wall to put in probable time sequence for whatever phase of the project they pertained to, we connected the sequenced tasks with string. Simple? *Yes.* Effective? *Yes.*

I helped plan numerous projects using the cards-and-string tool. It seemed that these projects had a higher rate of success than those I'd planned using complex project-management software tools. The significant difference in ratio of success probably resulted from the fact that the simple tools allowed more "true" participation from all people involved on the project than did the project-planning software tools (greater success undoubtedly because details necessary to planning the project were not subject to correction by the person—me—entering the data). The cards-and-string tool multiplied the effect of each person's contribution.

Based on my observations over time, I noticed that, say, three people working together on one project plan were not just three times more effective than one person funneling information from two others—three people frequently were *ten times* more effective than one person.

To this day, I continue to use project-management software tools. Now, however, I use them to record the plan *after* the group has created it using cards, tape, and string. Now when I need to plan a project, I use the computer as a recording-and-printing tool instead of as a "creating" tool.

My "discovery" of the effectiveness of the basic cards-tape-string planning technique inspired me to look for other simple tools—in particular for ones to use while gathering requirements during systems analysis, for modeling systems, and to use when designing systems—as well as for simple ways to improve upon the cards-tape-string technique.

Sticky notes came into my life as a big improvement over the index-cards method. As the universal fluid modeling tool, sticky notes remove the need for thumbtacks (thereby eliminating all those little holes in the wall) and eliminate much of the tackiness left behind by tape. I can write on a sticky note and place it on the wall without having to mess with tape and string. I can remove it and replace it with another one. I can create diagrams of ideas on a wall, and then, if the ideas are not arranged as I want, I can pull individual notes off and put them back on the wall in a different order or even somewhere else. I have posted sticky notes on a wall to design tiny projects on up to large and complex systems, including one $33 million group project. I have used them to outline sets of documents and even my first major book project, for which I had a lot of rearranging to do.

But I soon realized that even sticky notes on a wall could be improved upon. One simple improvement over posting notes directly on a wall is to stick them on a covering layer of butcher's paper or newsprint taped over the expanse of the wall. The beauty of this is that the rolls of paper are transportable. Once I've put all the sticky notes in order on this paper, I can pull the entire sheet off the wall, roll it up, and take it to display at another working meeting. Like the cheater pipes we used back at the asphalt plant, simple bits of paper can serve as tools to help get you through complexity.

LEARNING THROUGH EXPERIENCE

Although effective tools and techniques can be learned from seminars and textbooks, some of the most useful ones have probably never been documented. Take cheater pipes, for example. I've never read about cheater pipes anywhere, but everyone at the asphalt plant knew about them, and I've met several people in the years since who also knew about and used them. Perhaps there is some hidden, cheater-pipe user group out there.

Knowing that effective tools may be out there even though they're not described in standard textbooks has helped me on many occasions. I have spent much of my professional life writing computer programs. Textbooks provide scads of information on computer programming, but I have learned most useful techniques by seeing how other people write code and use tools. People learn skills in different ways but *I* learn more and faster by watching someone perform a task than I learn by reading a textbook on how to perform it. If I watch a peer use a code fragment successfully, for example, I tend to have confidence in the code and am likely to use it.

My preferred way of learning is called experiential learning, and I discovered how powerful this type of learning can be from the noted author, consultant, and teacher Jerry Weinberg (*see* [WEI-WEB]). I attended one of Jerry's training classes in which he assigned the class an exercise designed to help analysts better identify user requirements. Jerry divided the class into small working groups, and then gave each group a piece of paper containing his requirements for building a house.

This was not to be an ordinary stick-and-mortar house, however; this was to be a house of cards, and each group was to spend one hour building the house according to the requirements. At the end of the hour, we reconvened to show what we had built and to discuss the requirements. As you may have suspected, no one house of cards resembled another, and it occurred to me during the discussion that I should have sat with the user (Jerry, that is) and talked through the requirements word by word so that I would understand what he wanted instead of what I *interpreted* each requirement to mean.

Although I already knew from reading books that an analyst is supposed to validate requirements with the user, I didn't do what I knew. The lesson Jerry communicated with that assignment has stayed with me to this day because I *experienced it,* much as I experienced using cheater pipes.

The lesson to be learned from the fact that many simple tools are not described in standard textbooks is that the odds are good that there are more useful tips to be learned from practitioners than from books. Most important, use what works—for you, for your coworkers, for your staff, and for your customers, according to each person's preferred way to learn.

A Change Tool

Change occurs frequently in organizations, but we often choose expensive and ineffective ways to introduce and integrate it. For example, one method is to have a "change day." Frequently scheduled when the goal of the change is to improve process or practices, change days are announced by senior managers who declare that changeover day is coming. They bring in guest speakers who pronounce the virtue of the improvements the organization is seeking. These speakers are sincere and well meaning, and their speeches are motivating and instructive. The idea is that everyone will hear the speeches on change day, will go home at the end of the day, and then will return the next day to do things the "new" way—and all will perform their jobs better because of it.

Change days are expensive for myriad reasons. First, expert speakers do not come cheap. Second, the audience itself is expensive: Everyone in the organization stops work for a day to gather for the speeches. Product does not get produced or shipped, sales do not get closed, projects do not move forward, and the backlog of uncompleted tasks grows even more daunting.

The biggest expense, however, comes in the wake of change day. Although some people will have been convinced to do things differently and will dive into the fray heart and soul, they'll do so with only a little knowledge gained from change day. Other people will not have been convinced about the merit of the particular change. Such people—whether overtly or covertly—tend to resent change and the implication that they have not done things well enough already. They'll work to keep things as they are, with the result of change day being lots of effort and little productive change.

There is a more affordable and effective tool for bringing about change than change day. It is the idea that *change happens one person at a time*. Managers from the organization show one person at a time the benefit of doing things differently, giving individuals the knowledge and skills they'll need to perform tasks in the changed environment.

This approach is cheaper than running a change day because it does not require that motivational speakers be brought in, and it does not cause work to stop company-wide. Such an approach to change is not easy—change never is easy—but it is effective because the people who'll do the work are shown how to make the change.

Thoughts on the Cheater Pipe

I liked using the cheater pipe at the asphalt plant. It was a creative, practical, and inexpensive way to solve an ever-present problem, a kind of secret of the ages that helped us do things we couldn't otherwise do easily. We were using the laws of physics to accomplish a task cheaply and with good results. All we needed was some knowledge (torque equals force times length of lever), some creativity (fitting a left-over, six-foot-long pipe over a wrench handle), and some initiative (holding the contraption fast to each corroded nut and bolt while stretched out backside-down on concrete and grit). It also needed a manager who would allow us to "cheat" with a souped-up wrench.

By letting people use their knowledge, creativity, and initiative, we as managers may discover that there are more ways than one to get the job done.

THE HARD HAT

My first day on the job at the asphalt plant, I was issued a flat-point shovel and a hard hat. I wore my hard hat whenever I went outdoors. It was the rule to wear it, but I also wanted to wear it.

I must admit that I didn't want to wear a hard hat when I first started working. For one thing, the hat was made of plastic and was supremely uncomfortable. I had always thought that hard hats were made of some kind of metal. Didn't John Wayne wear a metal hard hat in one of his movies? And Jimmy Stewart, too? Heroes in those good-old classics wouldn't wear plastic. What good could plastic do?

For another thing, the hard hat made going outdoors in bad weather miserable. Even though my hat didn't sit directly on my head—a wide, plastic band fit snug against my forehead, leaving an air space between the top of my head and the hat—it trapped bucketfuls of perspiration on my head in summer and permitted cold wind in during winter. Louisiana winters are not like those in Wisconsin, but they aren't like those in Miami Beach either. That hard hat was torture both summer and winter.

Another reason I didn't like wearing the hard hat was that it didn't keep up with me. I could never adjust the headband so that the hat stayed securely in place. When I started walking, I felt as if my hat was half a step behind me. When I stopped, the hard hat kept going, sliding forward to a precarious slant.

Despite what I thought about wearing that hat, I wore it every minute I was outdoors, following company rules, no matter how useless I thought it was.

And then one day my attitude changed. I saw a laborer who wasn't wearing a hard hat crawl under the conveyor belts and machinery. Just as I was about to look around the yard for an extra hard hat, the guy appeared to cramp and suddenly reared up, slamming the top of his head full-force into the machinery. It was a hard hit, maybe not so hard that he saw stars like they do in the cartoons, but I could see that it hurt. The expression on that man's face was just what I needed to appreciate the value of the hard hat.

That bump on *his* head taught me

You don't always realize the worth of the tools you use.

INFRASTRUCTURE AS A TOOL

I had come to think of the hard hat as an invisible tool. I didn't really believe that I was using a tool that would save me from pain and agony, but I was. After I saw that bump on the head, an invisible tool became visible.

Through the years, I have come across other tools that, like the hard hat, were present without my realizing their worth. Most of the time, they were both present *and essential.* One way I've become aware of these essential yet invisible tools is by going places they are not present. For example, Nigeria. I lived in Lagos, Nigeria, for two years, from January, 1995, until December, 1996.

Lagos is a tropical port city located on both the mainland and an island off the southern coast of West Africa. It was for many years the capital of Nigeria, the country with the largest population of all African countries and home to one-fifth of the people living on the African continent. In the mid-1980s, Lagos had a population of approximately one million people. Today's population is estimated at fifteen million, and demographers predict that in twenty years, Lagos will have the largest population of any city on the planet. What it doesn't have is a modern, maintained infrastructure that people in developed countries take for granted.

Nigeria is an oil-producing country, with riches to spend on building a modern infrastructure—adequate electricity, potable water, accessible air and ground transportation, telecommunications. The considerable problem in Nigeria is that whatever infrastructure has been built, it has not been maintained.

Computers, telecommunications, cooling, and lighting all depend on electricity. During our years in Lagos, the power was on only about 60 to 70 percent of the time, but when it was on, tsunami-size surges were inevitable. The light bulbs in our kitchen, for example, would brighten, dim, brighten, dim, brighten, brighten, *brighten*—until the bulbs burst, sending glass shards to the floor.

Getting access to fresh, clean water was also a problem in Lagos. The infrastructure of pipes, purification plants, and pumps necessary to convey potable water to Lagos's entire population had been built, but without the necessary care and maintenance, the system just didn't work. The liquid that came out of our kitchen tap was often dirty. We had to filter and boil water before drinking it, cooking with it, or washing with it. We could always tell which people were new to Nigeria by the brightness of the shirts they wore to work. Anyone who had been in Lagos for six months had dingy shirts.

Another tool I'd taken for granted most of my life that was lacking in Lagos was telephone service. Telephones worked most of the time . . . if you had a working line connected. The line to our house wandered away several times when telephone workers cut the line between the pole and our house and reconnected it to someone else's house. Even without a working phone, we sometimes received a bill from the phone company for long-distance calls to other countries—bills that were in the neighborhood of $500 a month. Try to straighten out that infrastructure problem!

When we did have access to a working telephone, sometimes the phone would ring quietly or with two rings in close succession, which meant that a neighbor's line was being called and that we could not use the line until the other call was completed. Sometimes, my wife or I would pick up our phone to make a call and would hear a conversation in the background. Fortunately, we could put our call through and have *our conversation*, all the while hearing that faint other conversation in the background. I know that this crossed-wires thing happens in developed countries from time to time, but in Lagos, it was pretty much the norm, not the exception.

The local phone system was responsible for other challenging experiences during our years in Lagos. Take, for example, Internet dial-up. Maybe half the calls we dialed either did not go through or did not stay connected. Phone lines would drop out, and the computer would disconnect, so we would have to try again, and again, . . . and again. Even when the computer could connect and stay connected, the quality of the connection made conducting business close to impossible. The idea of using a 56kb connection never entered anyone's mind. On a good day, a 28.8kb connection might exist, but on most days, the best we could hope for would be something like 9,600 baud, or less.

But the most important tool that was missing from life in Nigeria took time for me to notice. The first clue should have been the large number of banks in Lagos—one on every other corner throughout the city. Nigeria is rich as a nation, but its people are poor, with a good salary being the equivalent of about one U.S. dollar a day. There were far too many banks for a city whose people earned so little.

A second clue came from the American Embassy, which warned Americans never to use a credit card anywhere in Nigeria. Most high-end stores and restaurants accepted credit cards, so it was tempting to throw warning to the wind. The reason behind the warning, however, was chilling: Credit card fraud was—and is to this day—rampant. When someone anywhere in Nigeria (but especially in Lagos and on Lagos Island) paid using a credit card, information from that card would be wired within the hour to one of the credit-card taker's many accomplices throughout the World, with the accomplice using the information to buy as much merchandise as possible, usually charging merchandise worth thousands of dollars within a day.

After just a month in Lagos, I could see evidence of fraud and theft everywhere—from the president (at the time, a military dictator) to government officials to waiters in restaurants. It was a fact that many government officials were corrupt to the point of not paying their employees. Instead, they kept the payroll for themselves, which explained the abundance of banks: People laundered money and used the banks to send it to accounts in Switzerland and other parts of the World.

The crumbling infrastructure was accelerated by the rampant fraud. The telephone worker whose employer was not paying him the salary due to him would disconnect phone lines allocated to existing customers and reconnect them to serve people who would bypass the employer and pay him directly. He did this in order to feed himself and his family. At power, water, and other utilities, workers who were not being paid by their employers would sell maintenance materials on the black market. Police and other law-enforcement personnel who weren't being paid stopped cars on the street and took money from the drivers and passengers.

The effect of fraud on the population was devastating but, arguably, the most important contributor to the misery experienced by people at all levels of Nigerian society was a *lack of trust*, the invisible component that allows people to abide by common rules and practices in order to function without always having to watch their backs. When trust is not present, no amount of planning, managerial oversight, or technical expertise can make things right.

CHANGING PERSPECTIVES

My professional and personal experiences in Nigeria so contrasted what I was used to back home that I increasingly became more aware of other invisible tools that I previously had taken for granted. Changing my environment in such a dramatic fashion allowed me to see tools I hadn't realized I was using. Changes I made at other times during my early career were less drastic, but they also caused me to notice invisible tools.

For example, during the latter half of the 1990s, I worked in a group of engineers and project managers. In the beginning, we had a support staff of secretaries and administrative assistants but, as the years went by, our senior managers moved responsibility for performing these tasks from the support staff to us—the engineers and project managers. Senior managers provided us with auto-mated tools so that we could make our own travel arrangements, submit expense accounts, enroll in training courses, submit train-ing budgets, allocate money to contracts, pay contract vouchers, and so on. Senior management favored this change because it saved a significant amount of money by not paying salaries to phased-out support staff members, whose payroll generally exceeded the combined cost of purchasing automated tools and then training the engineers and project managers to use the tools.

Travel tasks were the first tasks to be automated. Prior to automation, I used to scribble my itinerary on a scrap of paper and hand it to a secretary. I could express my preferences in as much or as little detail as I wanted. What I didn't specify, the secretary would supply, using her best judgment. I had no clear idea of what the secretary did after getting my itinerary or of how much effort she needed to devote to making all the arrangements, but I always had my tickets on time and each hotel had a room for me when I arrived. The secretaries were so wonderful at doing their job that I was oblivious to the details.

I did come to appreciate how much help the secretaries had given us when senior managers forced us to perform this work ourselves—it was then that I understood that our secretaries had been a human form of tool, enabling us to do our jobs better. Without them to assist me, I sat endless hours at my computer, typing in my trip plans and expense reports, using the automated tool's online form. I didn't like having to enter all the necessary information. One reason I was especially unhappy was because the automated tool would not accept my preferences in as little or as much detail as I wanted to give. Rather than leaving gaps for the secretaries to fill in or select, I had to enter details about all aspects of my planned trip, and I had to follow the tool's precise format. When I returned from each trip, I then had to enter expense details. What a colossal pain.

From these and similar experiences I had working with travel and accounting tools, I learned about the importance of making tools visible. Plenty of emotion is involved in learning you are using a tool that you heretofore have been oblivious to using. Forcing people to change tools may be good for them in some ways, but it does no good to tell people that a change will be for the better, as our managers did, because they will discover otherwise. Changing people's perspective is what matters.

TOOLS? WHAT TOOLS? MAKING TOOLS VISIBLE

Thinking about the visibility of tools and the role played by changing perspective led me to analyze how I do things at work. At the beginning of every new task, whether small and seemingly manageable or large and predictably complex, I ask myself four questions, having discovered that the answers help me to better understand the work that lies ahead.

First I ask, *"How do I see invisible tools?"*

Noticing tools that I have previously been oblivious to isn't easy. The best way I've found to make these tools visible is to think about what happens to this object—or this piece of my work—after it leaves my hands and goes to another person—or to an automated system—for handling. By thinking about how that other person or automated system does the job, I make myself more aware of the value of the tool. For example, if my work depends on some type of automated system that I use every day, thinking about who maintains the system makes an aspect of it more visible to me.

The second question I ask is, *"Why are invisible tools invisible?"*

Most invisible tools probably were visible at some point in the past. Someone at some time decided to make them invisible. Understanding the reason why that someone changed the tool's visibility can teach me things about the tool, about the people using it, and about how I use it.

At one of my jobs, secretaries continued to make travel arrangements even when the engineers had both the ability and the tools to make arrangements for themselves. The reason secretaries made the arrangements was that the engineers' managers in that workplace traveled a lot themselves and didn't want to do this task for themselves. So, the engineers rode on the managers' coattails, so to speak, when it came to making travel arrangements.

Understanding why a tool is invisible allows you to give informed input when making future decisions about that tool. The reasons that lead to a decision about a tool will change with respect to a work environment. If I understand those reasons and can recognize change in them, I can make sure the best—not necessarily the least expensive—decision is made.

Many tools I use in the workplace are visible, and so the third question I consider is the converse of the previous question: *"Why are visible tools visible?"*

One answer is that visible tools tend to be low quality, awkward, and confusing to use. Those negative aspects make people notice the tool. The automated tool I first used to arrange my travel plans and to report my travel expenses was irritatingly awkward, the sequence in which information need to be entered was not intuitive to me, and the instructions were confusing, as if translated from a foreign language in the stilted fashion of such things. I knew I was using an inferior tool.

Tools also are visible that are versatile and bring great benefit. The front-end loader I learned to operate at the asphalt plant was one such tool, visible not just because it was a physical object that could be touched, but visible in the more important sense that it was so useful—we used that front-end loader for a multitude of tasks.

If I make a versatile and beneficial tool invisible, I risk losing the use of it. This unhappy consequence is especially probable if the tool is a living, breathing human being. On one project I led years ago, a man named Frank did his work quickly and expertly. Because he was so exemplary at doing every task asked of him, Frank was *visible*, standing out from the rest of the staff. If I had not shown Frank how greatly I appreciated his accuracy and the professional approach he took to doing his job—that is, had I taken him for granted and assumed that he would always be there— Frank undoubtedly would have left my staff to go work for a more deserving boss. Had I not given Frank the appreciation I communicated regularly to him, I would have made a visible tool invisible, and that would have been so much more than foolish.

The fourth question I consider is, *"Will changing the visible/invisible state of the tool bring benefit?"*

Studies have shown that change in the workplace generally brings a short-term benefit in the form of increased worker productivity *(for more on this topic, see* [DEM90], [DEM99] and [DEM08]). For example, workers typically will try harder when using a new approach, thereby potentially increasing productivity. The effect change has on work is known as the Hawthorne effect.

Automating a task previously performed manually by a person (for example, automating so that I can make my own travel arrangements rather than wait for them to be done by a secretary) helps me to better appreciate the work and value of that person and makes an invisible tool visible to me. Gaining a better appreciation of coworkers is a fine reason for making a change, but managers need to be careful about the manner in which change is introduced, primarily because many people lose steam when someone or something else forces them to do things for themselves that previously were done for them.

I, for one, like personal services and feel disenfranchised, grumpy, and even resentful when managers take them away, but a short-term and temporary removal of them helps me better appreciate the people as a visible tool performing the service. By trying to understand the reason why I use a particular tool and why it is best to keep one tool visible and another invisible, I hope to improve the way I do my work as well as the way I manage others.

Understanding why one society strives to have water pipes bring potable water to homes and businesses, why some businesses employ secretaries and loading-dock workers, and even why a college kid on the job at an asphalt plant should don an uncomfortable plastic hat in summer and winter helps me understand work and the people at work. It also helps me improve the work when situations change.

Thoughts on the Hard Hat

I still have my hard hat from my days at the asphalt plant. Somehow, it has traveled with me through all the changes I have experienced in my life in the past twenty-five years. I rarely wear it as it is still too hot in the summer and too cold in the winter, but seeing it on the corner shelf reminds me to look for tools I use without having realized they are tools—useful, versatile, beneficial, visible and invisible tools.

I did wear my hard hat in the office once—at a Halloween costume party held the year the parking garage was being built right outside my office window. For the party, I dressed as a construction worker, inspired by the real deal laboring outside my window and egged on by some of my organization's female employees (most of whom had spent a fair amount of time gazing out my window at those workers, searching for one who came even close to looking like the well-built, ruggedly handsome actor who had appeared in a recent series of Diet Coke commercials!). I won first prize in the costume contest (no real surprise there as these same ladies were the judges) and sauntered around the party drinking diet colas, wearing my hard hat, work boots, and a pair of faded-denim overalls left over from a spell helping out on my family's Louisiana farm.

The experience was fun for this introverted and not-so-rugged engineer, but not everyone enjoyed the party. One senior manager hid himself in his office behind a tightly closed door, appearing every so often with a long face and hunched over like the weight of the Universe was on his shoulders. Perhaps he wanted everyone to think that he had too much responsibility to party, but I think he missed an opportunity to build goodwill, an invisible tool the value of which is most evident when it disappears. A Halloween costume party at work doesn't cost much money, but it can bring benefit to the workplace in the form of levity and strengthened relationships. For me, such events are like hard hats at the asphalt plant: They are mostly invisible, can be uncomfortable for many of us, but are remarkably good tools.

CONCLUSIONS

I used a variety of tools before going to work at the asphalt plant, but it was there that I realized that I had less knowledge and experience with tools than I had thought. I do believe that I learned more about physics and physical tools in my four years working part-time at the plant than I have learned during the ensuing years. The physical tools at the plant helped me learn about other types of tools and how to use them in other places and other ways.

The life-lessons I learned with and about tools are

When the environment is changed, the tool may need to be changed.

The simplest things can multiply effectiveness.

You don't always realize the worth of the tools you use.

REFERENCES

[DEM90]   See, for example, "Cleanroom Software Development" by R.W. Selby, V.R. Basili, and F.T. Baker, copyright © 1987 IEEE, reprinted in *Software State of the Art: Selected Papers*, T. DeMarco and T.R. Lister, eds. (New York: Dorset House Publishing, 1990), pp. 256-76.

[DEM99]   T. DeMarco and T. Lister, *Peopleware: Productive Projects and Teams,* 2nd ed. (New York: Dorset House Publishing, 1999).

[DEM08]   T. DeMarco, et al., *Adrenaline Junkies and Template Zombies: Understanding Patterns of Project Behavior* (New York: Dorset House Publishing, 2008).

[WEIWEB]   See www.geraldmweinberg.com.

TWO

Raw Materials

Raw materials are in front of every one of us every day. The trouble is, seeing their value isn't always easy. As managers, we can work more effectively (and similarly guide those we manage) if we notice which raw materials are available and see their value. From my experience with raw materials at the asphalt plant, I learned some surprising management principles.

There were thousands of tons of raw materials at the plant. Materials were so plentiful that I took little notice of them most of the time, but slowly and surely, I realized what important, beneficial properties the materials possessed. With time, I discovered that materials that are both at hand and in good supply can be used in a multitude of ways. Noticing the materials and finding good uses for them were my challenge.

I learned that some of the better uses are often unexpected. Rocks, I found out, are good for cooking. That's right—rocks can cook. I, in fact, enjoyed delicious hot lunches at the plant, thanks to the heat generated by plain, old, dirty (but hot) rocks.

Working with raw materials at the asphalt plant helped me to see that it is valuable to understand what is important in one's surroundings and what is not. Some raw materials are worthless in many respects. What is key is to understand that one seemingly worthless raw material may become exceedingly valuable when used for a specific task.

The challenge for managers is to utilize raw materials in situations in which they perform best. As a manager, I focus on developing the raw material *in the people* I work with everyday. I don't have to make people perfect—it might be nice, but it really doesn't matter—I just need to link capabilities with getting the job done.

Much of what I saw and experienced working with raw materials at the asphalt plant was unexpected. For example, I found some semi-precious jewels in the thousands of tons of rocks, sand, and dirt that went scudding by me each day. Distant cousins of many of those gems presumably had gone unnoticed for many years, but for some reason, I was able to see the precious materials in front of me much more clearly than others working at the plant had done. From the experience, I learned to look closely at the potential to be developed in raw materials, and I encourage you to see the raw material in your people so as to put it to good use much sooner than I did.

COOKING WITH ROCKS

With two main heaters, an asphalt plant generates an impressive amount of heat. The asphalt heater (the smaller of the two heaters) burns a low-grade diesel fuel oil to keep the liquid asphalt hot so that it is at the right consistency for mixing with the rocks, dirt, and sand. The asphalt heater heats pipes in a large tank filled with liquid asphalt. The heater heats the pipes, which in turn heat the liquid asphalt.

The second, larger heater is housed in a machine called "the dryer." Because rocks, sand, and dirt at the asphalt plant are often wet, the dryer has to be used to dry them. If wet rocks or droplets of water ever were to touch the liquid asphalt, the combination could cause the mixture to explode. (You've probably experienced something like this at home if you ever accidentally sprinkled even just a few drops of water in hot oil. The drama when you are cooking at home is considerably different from that at the asphalt plant, but you can see that little drops of water in hot oil can cause little explosions. Now, imagine doing this with thousands of gallons of oil and water. *Kaboom!*)

The dryer looks like a home clothes dryer except that it is really big—about fifteen feet in diameter and about fifty feet long. A large engine spins and tilts the dryer while gravity pulls dirt, sand, and rocks through it. The fuel-oil burner, about twelve inches in diameter, shoots a large flame into the dryer. The materials come out of the dryer dry and hot—400° F. The result of using the dryer is tons of rocks heated to 400° F.

Every now and then, a small pile of hot rocks ("small" being about two hundred pounds) would accumulate on the ground, either by nuisance or by design. The nuisance occurred when we had an imbalance of materials in the part of the asphalt plant that mixed the hot and dry materials with the liquid asphalt. When this happened, generally several times a day, the asphalt plant operator would need to flush the mixer and drop the hot rocks out of the bottom. This was a considerable nuisance in that we had to stop whatever job we were doing and clean out the imbalance of materials.

The asphalt plant operator could generate the same result *by design* if what workers wanted was a pile of hot rocks. By manipulating the mixer to stop the flow of all materials except rocks, the operator could then drop the rocks to form a hot-rock pile below the asphalt plant.

So, what did we want with a pile of 400° F rocks? We wanted to cook! Cold ham-and-cheese sandwiches are mighty good sometimes, but most times, nothing satisfies so much as a piping-hot, freshly cooked, full-blown meal. Sometimes, all I cooked was a simple piece of meat, but more often than not, I cooked a complete meal.

Preparation started before I left my house in the morning. I would season a hamburger patty or a piece of fish or chicken and double-wrap it in aluminum foil. Then, I'd drop the parcel in my lunch box along with some bread and a couple of freezer packs to keep the food from spoiling in the hot Louisiana air. About half an hour before lunch break, we'd ask the asphalt plant operator to dump a load of hot rocks into a pile that could be scooped up by the front-end loader and moved out of the way as we continued to work. To cook my food, I would make a hollow in the pile of hot rocks, place the wrapped food in the hollow, and shovel more hot rocks over it to cover. About thirty minutes later, I'd pull my parcel from the rock pile, put the freshly cooked food in the bun or French bread I'd packed for myself, and I'd have myself a juicy, hot sandwich.

Even better was when I made a complete-plate lunch. To do this, I'd put cooked fish or meat, some leftover cooked potatoes or rice, and a sprinkling of frozen or canned veggies (just for good measure) on a metal pie plate. I'd wrap it twice in foil and put it in my lunch box with the necessary freezer packs. When lunchtime drew near, I'd pop the parcel into the pile of hot rocks. Half an hour in the rocks and a good, hot lunch was ready. With hot rocks at hand, who needs a microwave oven?

Before working at the plant, I would have thought cooking lunch in a pile of dirty rocks pretty disgusting. After all, how could rocks that had been churning around inside an asphalt plant be sanitary enough to consider using for the preparation of food— my food, at that? (Okay, so I was never much of a Boy Scout or summer-camper who cooked foil-wrapped food over a wood or charcoal campfire.) Let me assure you, however, disgusting this method was not. The hot meals were a treat and the rocks I cooked meals with taught me that

Stuff that is lying around can be quite useful.

Or, to put the sentiment another way:

One man's rubbish may be another man's treasure.

EMPTY BOXES

On one job during my early career, I worked just down the hall from the office responsible for the care and feeding of the many printers in the building. At least once a week, my hall-mates would set out an empty printer-paper box. Most people didn't pay much attention to this because it was such a common sight—the office threw out about one-hundred-and-fifty empty boxes a year.

I noticed, however, because after a while, I viewed those empty boxes as a solution to one of the biggest problems I had in that job: clutter. I had spare parts, cables, and tools scattered across shelves, desks, and tables, with still more stuff piled in drawers and cabinets and stacked high on my credenza. Although the whole, disorganized mess distressed me considerably (I have been called a neat-nik more than once or twice in my life), I could almost tolerate the mess. For me, the bigger problem was that the mess was causing me to waste time and money.

Situations would arise when I needed a specific part that I knew was there somewhere, but I couldn't find it. Then, I was forced to buy the part new. Even worse were the times when a colleague would come from some distance to work with me and we'd need a specific cable to send back with him or her to continue work at the remote job site. When the cable couldn't be located, I'd have to buy a new one and also pay for shipping it to the remote site. That infuriated me because in addition to being a neat-nik, I'm also thrifty—and I don't like spending my own or the government's money when clutter is at the root of the evil.

So I quickly learned to see the empty boxes as plentiful resources—like the rocks at the asphalt plant—and put them to work to hold and help organize my spare parts. This was good. I now knew what I had on hand *and where I had put it.* I also seemed to have more storage space than before. Better organization and more space were nice, but the payoff was that I no longer wasted time and money buying parts that I already had.

Extra People

One of the resources organizations have that may be surprisingly underutilized is staff. Conventional wisdom teaches us that people are expensive—in terms of salary, training, benefits, and managerial oversight—and organizations don't want extra people on the payroll who are not being fully utilized. The smart manager sees ways to use such staff members by moving them to jobs where their skill sets and personal attributes will matter.

In the mid-eighties, I worked in a computer lab where we struggled with configuration management—a task that is not complex in a technical sense, but many people find it boring and do not like to do it. That was the problem at the lab—until our manager noticed that Jim, a contractor working in security administration, was about to be replaced by a government employee returning to the project after an extensive leave.

Our manager had admired the diligence and discipline Jim had shown as he performed in the security-administration position, and knew he would do what people asked him to do, performing meticulous, detailed, boring jobs that other people avoided.

Jim had never done configuration-management work, and he had no training in the field. He did, however, have the personal qualities that our manager believed would enable him to carry out the configuration-management responsibilities for our critical project. Utilizing Jim in this fashion was a major success: He completed every task on time, noted every detail, and filed every report. Even better, he discovered several problems in the project in time for us to correct them, thereby helping the project to succeed.

GROWING PEOPLE

Using an abundance of hot rocks or cardboard boxes in ways that are different from what they were procured for illustrates how tools can be given a kind of second life. It also illustrates that tools can come from anywhere.

Applying this idea to the real world of managing work presents a different sort of challenge: How can managers take advantage of an abundance of hot rocks or empty boxes to improve productivity and employee satisfaction as people do their work?

If this sounds puzzling, please read on: Imagine coming with me to my job where I am a busy manager. The people who work for me are also busy. We all work long, difficult days just to hold back an onslaught of work. What I have in abundance is work to do and people who work hard.

By sharing my abundance of tasks with people who are accustomed to working long and hard, I provide them with work that is new and challenging to them. Here, I state this concept in basic, almost simplistic terms, but the task of "growing people" is itself neither basic nor simplistic. Many people struggle with the new work at first, but in the vast majority of cases, people given the challenge learn how to do the new work and grow both as employees and people.

LOOKING FOR HOT ROCKS

It became obvious to me at the asphalt plant that hot rocks could heat anything that touched them. Most of the places I have worked have had the equivalent of hot rocks. By considering the abundant clutter of your work environment and the resources you need to improve your work, you may find that they are one and the same.

The first step I take is to make a list of the resources I find. I write the name of each item on a large sheet of paper or on a white board, and note what use I'll have for the item next to it.

My second step is to create a list of problems in the workplace. This isn't hard to do as I usually have my own list of small and big things I would do differently. I also listen to others as they grumble about what bothers them on the average day. At the asphalt plant, for example, we all grew tired of eating cold food at lunch and saw the rocks as a way to have hot food.

The third step I take is to examine my list of resources and my list of problems, and then I try to match the resources as solutions to the problems. Sometimes, the match is easy to see: The heat in the rocks matched with our desire for hot food. Sometimes, the match is there, but not obvious. I did *not* notice that Jim could be the right match to do configuration-management work, but someone else did.

This three-step process is simple, but it is not always easy. Matches rarely come in a few minutes or even hours. I recommend keeping the lists on paper placed in a safe but accessible desk drawer or on a white board that will not be needed for another purpose. I add the names of resource items when they pop into my head, sometimes at odd times when I am not even aware I am searching. Matching resources and needs also tends to occur when I least expect it, so it is important to have the lists accessible.

USING HOT ROCKS

I was staring at my first computer monitor years ago and noticed waves of heat rising from it. Aha! Computer monitors generate heat—not enough to burn my finger, but the rising air is warm to the touch. Heat is a resource, but what need might I identify?

Heat from that monitor was nothing like the heat generated by the hot rocks at the plant, but it occurred to me that I could use it for a similar purpose—to help defrost the homemade frozen dinners I sometimes bring to work for lunch. When frozen hard, they take a long time to heat evenly in the office's low-powered microwave oven, but setting the frozen dinner on top of the computer monitor for a few hours before lunch thaws it. Once thawed, it is easy to heat evenly in the microwave.

Enough about food—here's an office-space-saver example: The ceiling in my office is eight-feet high, with three to five feet between the top of most pieces of standard-issue furniture and the ceiling. My office, like most of the cubicles and offices in that building, is exceedingly cramped. Everyone complains about it, but no one does much to correct the problem. One morning when I was pushing my desk against the wall to try to get myself a bit more space, I suddenly experienced an *Aha!*

At that moment, it occurred to me that if I replaced some of the furniture in my office with tall, narrow pieces, I could make better use of the space, claiming air-rights, just as developers in heavily populated urban areas such as New York City have long done with the space above low buildings. First, I replaced my two three-drawer file cabinets with one narrow, seven-drawer cabinet. Then, I replaced the double-width, four-foot-tall bookcase with a narrower, seven-foot-tall set of shelves.

When I finished, clients and vendors visiting our offices wondered how I'd managed to get a larger office than everyone else. My office, of course, was the same size as everyone else's, but I had reconfigured it to use the space more constructively, matching my preferences and needs with a previously underutilized resource.

I found another way to apply the hot-rocks philosophy in my current office, which has scads of bare walls. People on the project were having a difficult time getting their message across to others on the project and to management. Project staff members wanted to share information about their work, but they didn't want to disrupt their own and other people's concentration and progress to discuss every little and big matter. We had all talked informally about ways to get around what seemed to be interminable one-on-one powwows and digressions, but we didn't seem to have a good way to address the real need.

Then one day, digging through a closet, I found several boxes containing large, white, plastic sheets of a kind designed to cling to any clean, flat surface by means of static charge—another *Aha!* This material was just the thing we needed to turn those bare walls into interactive centers for project communication. The plastic sheets would adhere to the walls without our having to use adhesive—adhesive being a major no-no with building maintenance!— and project artifacts could be taped to the sheets where everyone could see them. I encouraged project members to write everything they could think of related to our current project on these plastic cling sheets before and after they were static-clung on the walls. This simple product vastly improved our ability to share information and to perform the work we needed to do to move our project forward.

But what's really important on a project are *people.* People in every organization play a specified role at work, and many play multiple roles, but there is much more to each of us than what role we fill at work. For example, coworkers and bosses and secretaries and maintenance workers are diverse—just like you and me. They cook, play guitar, tell jokes, soothe feelings, mow lawns, raise children, and do many other things that we don't normally associate with work.

What is important to understand from this diversity is that most people are willing to do unusual tasks *on the job* if we provide the context for our request and if we properly compensate them for jobs done above and beyond what their normal salary covers. There are times, unfortunately, when the difference between the success or failure of a project may be one key person working late or working weekends. Matching the person—our resource—with the project—our need—looks straightforward on paper, but the problem arises when that key person cannot put in the extra time because he or she has personal commitments to attend to evenings and weekends, such as taking the car for an oil change, waiting for a repairman to fix the furnace, or driving a child from school to soccer practice.

The wise manager is one who can keep the goals of the key person—and also the goals of *each* individual on the staff—as much in mind as the goals of the project. Such a manager may actively work to help locate people—perhaps even another project member—who, for the short term, can take over some or all of these personal tasks for the key person. This action can be taken *only* if we appreciate the surrogates, use their abilities, and pay them well for their time.

Be careful, however, if considering this action as a "solution." Asking one staff member to substitute for another cannot be thought of as one person doing a *favor* for another. Tasks such as serving the project by driving another project member's children to a soccer game or house-sitting while the furnace is repaired are not in the job description of anyone I know, but people can and are willing to do such jobs for another person *under certain circumstances and if we pay them.* We need to recognize, however, that what "if we pay them" means is that *we need to pay them at the same rate they earn doing their normal day job.*

I've noted "if we pay them" several times in the preceding discussion. Matching project resources with project needs can be surprisingly complicated and may mean that compensation for project work performed in the office and compensation for work done to satisfy another's personal commitments contribute equally to the success (or failure) of the project.

Thoughts on Cooking With Rocks

Once I learned the secret of cooking with hot rocks, I began to notice and use other sources of heat at the asphalt plant. On the rare cold days, I could put my foil-wrapped parcel of food on an electric heater. On other days, I could cook on an electric motor or on a recently parked dump truck's engine. I found many "cookers" scattered about the plant, but I have also found many other, free, abundant, and useful tools since then. In addition to wonderful tools like hot rocks and empty boxes, the tools I've treasured most in my life just might be great ideas that people are willing to share. All one has to do is look, ask, and use.

THE BUCK FOLDING KNIFE

When I worked at the asphalt plant, one of the items workers liked to carry around was a Buck folding knife. Buck is one of the more famous hunting-knife companies, and during the 1970s, the company made a folding knife with a four-inch blade, handles of wood, and brass trim. It came with a leather pouch that slid onto a belt, and for many reasons, workers at the plant held this particular knife in high regard.

Although prestige was probably the main reason most workers carried the Buck knife, there were some practical reasons, too. People would use it to slice an apple or peel an orange or to do repair work, such as trimming excess material from a conveyor belt or cutting off old fan belts in order to replace them with new belts.

I suppose there were more reasons for carrying the Buck off the job. Most workers lived in rural areas in homes built on a few acres of land, complete with garden plots and livestock. At homes like these, there was always some bailing twine to cut or feed sacks to open. The plant, however, was where the Buck reigned.

One reason for the knife's stellar reputation became evident to me during my early days at the plant. One of my fellow laborers had one of these Buck folding knives, and he carried it in a leather pouch he wore on his belt. He was proud both of his possession and of the fact that he had bought the expensive knife "barely used" from someone at half the price a new one would garner. Each day, he would pull out the knife to show it to anyone who had not yet seen it. He took every opportunity to remove the knife from the pouch and cut something, whether or not as part of the job. Within weeks, everyone at the plant knew about that knife on his belt.

One day, he and I were on the crew performing some maintenance that required us to turn a motor a half-turn by hand. Suddenly, he attempted this by grabbing a fan belt and pulling it. The belt pulled farther than anticipated, catching his fingers between the belt and a pulley wheel, slowly pulling his fingers into the trap. The motor would not reverse direction to free him, making it obvious—at least to those of us frozen in horror as we watched helplessly—that the pulley wheel was about to sever his fingers. With no time to spare, an experienced mechanic standing near the fan belt recognized what was happening and, in what seemed to be a single motion, pulled the Buck folding knife from the man's leather pouch, slashed the fan belt, and stopped the machinery dead.

Well, that one act, which made use of quick thinking and a common tool, saved a man's fingers and was, without a doubt, the most important use I'd ever seen anyone find for a knife. This taught me

The most important use of a tool may be the least expected.

EXPECTATIONS

The "usual" is something that occurs most of the time, day after day. Eventually, what might actually be distinctive about that something "usual" fades into the recesses of memory. For me, whatever is "usual" guides my decisions at work. Focusing on the usual to the exclusion of all else, however, can be harmful.

For example, if I optimize my tools and workplace to the point where something unusual dooms me, this is not a good outcome. Leaving a little wiggle room for handling the unexpected is a wiser strategy. When the unexpected happened that afternoon at the asphalt plant and my fellow laborer almost lost some fingers, I understood that seeing the unexpected can snap open the eyes of those expecting the usual. The event expanded my awareness of the realm of possibilities—possibilities in ways a situation instantaneously can change and in ways an everyday tool can be used. The event also showed me the difference between understanding what is "usually important" and being ready to do what is "really important" when the unusual occurs.

Discovering the "really important" when the unexpected occurs reversed the fortune of that one man at the plant, but it can work in similar ways with a whole group of people. A kind of reversal of fortune amazed me some years ago at a computer lab where I supervised a dozen programmers who had responsibility for writing and maintaining software that enabled a group of analysts to process signals. The analysts were the stars of the lab; we were the support people—and both sides *usually* performed their roles as expected. But not always—a situation brought painfully to light when the analysts complained bitterly about our performance as support programmers.

Believe me when I state that I took this criticism *to heart*. I suspected that I probably could not evaluate my own group's performance objectively, and so I invited a consultant to spend a few hours talking with groups of my programmers and managers—*and analysts*—in order to assess the software tools and processes we used, the programmers' credentials, and our relationship with the analysts.

Several weeks later, the consultant sent us his report—and recommendations for small changes that we subsequently implemented. The relationship between analysts and programmers in the lab did improve after the consultant's recommendations were implemented, but the primary reason for the improvement was not a result of the consultant's report. The primary reason relations improved was that the consultant focused attention on the concerns of the programmers, not just on those of the usual stars—the analysts.

As a result of the attention we received, we started taking greater care to write and maintain the software on a higher, more-professional level. We had known all along what was expected of us, but it took the consultant's report to help us see that we'd let our second-class-citizen image define the job we did. After we received the consultant's attention, we started behaving like professionals, and the results were improved self-esteem and greatly improved support to the analysts. Before the consultant visited, we knew that software performance was important. The really important thing, however, was self-esteem, brought to the surface by an unusual situation—a consultant's visit—and an unusual tool—the consultant.

DIVERSITY AND CONFORMITY

I don't just wait for the unexpected to shock me into change at work. I try always to be ready to learn from unexpected experiences and results. The best way to be ready is by being familiar with and watchful of the tools I use.

I frequently choose the tools I use at work. I always choose the tools I use at home. If I have an open mind and look for all possible uses, I am apt to look for diversity rather than uniformity in my tools. The advantages of diversity outweigh the disadvantages.

Despite my preference for looking for unexpected uses for tools, I do know that uniformity can improve efficiency. (Think of what the assembly line did for the auto industry.) When focusing on what an individual or an organization is trying to accomplish, one probably should concentrate on the core of the endeavor and stay with that core. When selecting tools to purchase, I certainly could focus only on what the tool was designed to do and restrict myself, say, to using a hammer only to pound nails into wood—but I see little to recommend that approach. Yes, I could probably do all my work while using tools that are simpler, cheaper, and more efficient than the ones I buy, but life-lessons are not to be learned from that.

Uniformity in tools makes people and organizations vulnerable, and, possibly, more susceptible to tragedy. When all tools are chosen to take me, as an individual, or my organization in one specific direction, a poorly chosen direction or a change of direction becomes a tool that can destroy the system.

Consider a computer programming shop where all the employees are people in their mid-twenties, with plenty of energy and drive. They can listen to a manager's motivational speech, be convinced of the worth of the direction advocated, and charge off with deep concentration to work for long hours. If the manager has chosen the wrong direction for the organization, this charge will take it right over a cliff.

If this hypothetical programming shop were populated by people all in their mid-forties, a similar tragedy could occur, but for a different reason. People in this group would have experience and wisdom. They would not be likely to be led off a cliff by a motivational speech from a manager. They will ponder and further discuss the situation before moving in the direction advocated—the tool—because, perhaps, they think they know better. The tragedy that awaits them may be that their reluctance to change direction quickly could hold them in a disastrous position if they are wrong and the manager is right.

The challenge is to employ diversity in the tools I choose. Diversity is not always as efficient as uniformity, but it ensures ways to do work that will leave the organization less vulnerable if the unexpected occurs. In the two groups of programmers, diversity could be accomplished by infusing a mixture of younger and older people into each group. The mixed group would have experience that would increase the chance of moving the organization in the right direction as well as enough energy for all to charge ahead once a direction is chosen.

Choosing diversity in tools can cost an organization more money. In the group of computer programmers, choosing uniformity and employing only younger programmers could cost less in salaries than mixing younger and older programmers together. One way to justify greater cost is to allocate it to research and development. Having different tools helps people to look at and learn from problems outside the core of an endeavor. Having some older people in a programming shop will allow an organization to bring past experience to new opportunities because older people can serve as an in-house resource for training the younger people. The reverse is also true: The younger people can teach their elders.

Another way to justify the cost of diversity is by considering it to be risk mitigation. In the field of risk management, a "risk" is a problem that may occur *but has not yet occurred*. Risk mitigation involves spending resources in anticipation of these potential problems. Diverse tools can handle situations that are out of the ordinary. By identifying risks, I point to one type of situation that is out of the ordinary *(see* [DEM03] *for an extensive discussion of risk management).*

Paying higher salaries to more-experienced workers often makes sense: They are better able to deal with unexpected situations because they have done so in the past.

OPEN EYES

I use tools at work every day to deal with the various situations I encounter. The vast majority of situations are usual and expected. It is my challenge to find the unexpected use of a tool for the unexpected situation.

The tools I find don't do the job by themselves. My additional challenge is to keep my eyes open and my thinking cap on. I first must understand what situations are "usual" in my organization; I next must think about what might occur that is "unexpected"— whether bad or good. If I keep my eyes open, I'll learn to anticipate what the unexpected situations are and what properties of my tools could be useful in such situations. To document my observations, I write them on lists, which I keep handy because I never know when the unexpected will occur. Whenever it does, I undoubtedly will discover another important use of a tool.

Thoughts on the Buck Folding Knife

I never owned one of those classic wood-and-brass Buck folding knives. I couldn't really afford one at the plant because I needed my laborer's salary to help pay for my college tuition, but later on, when I was working as an engineer, I did buy a lighter-weight, Buck folding knife, one with a synthetic handle.

The knife I bought is probably just as useful as the ones so many men used at the plant (although not nearly as handsome), and it was only the first of many knives I've purchased in my lifetime. I've come to realize how much the fan-belt episode contributed to my fascination with knives. Whenever I have the chance, I read books about knives and about knife-making. I even made a knife once, by gluing fancy handles onto a pre-formed blade and then shaping everything to fit my hand. Strangely enough, the fascination with knives runs in my family, too. My younger brother makes really good custom knives (*see* [PHIWEB]).

Knives are great for opening boxes and cans of food, a function that is especially important to someone nomadic who, like me, has moved in and out of foreign countries and from state to state and client to client. People who see me opening boxes of printer paper in the office usually comment on my knife and how adeptly I use it. Sometimes I take the time to tell the story about that day at the plant when a tool and a new use came together in a split second in an unanticipated way.

MAKING WRENCHES

Almost every other week, the crew at the asphalt plant spent a day performing maintenance. As I mentioned in the "Tools" chapter, maintenance days usually fell on Saturdays so that the plant could be up and running by Monday. Sometimes during maintenance, the entire crew (usually six to ten men) had to remove several hundred bolts from the asphalt plant. Each bolt was the same size, so we needed as many wrenches as we had men on the crew, and all the wrenches had to be the same size.

Buying ten identical wrenches was expensive because, back in those days anyway, the usual way wrenches were packaged for purchase was in sets of eight. Each set contained one wrench the size we needed and seven others in sizes we didn't need for that particular job. We would have had to buy eighty wrenches in order to get the ten identical wrenches we wanted, and that was just too expensive.

You'd think that the obvious thing to do would have been to go to the tool bin at the hardware store and buy ten identical wrenches that were just the right size. Back then, in my part of Louisiana, however, stores wouldn't sell wrenches that way.

So, a mechanic at the plant solved this problem by custom-making wrenches—the cheater pipes I wrote about in the previous chapter, but my point here is different, so please bear with me. In this case, the mechanic fashioned wrenches that were actually "wrench-less." He would collect junk steel piping and tubes from a scrap pile, cut the steel piping to a uniform length, and then cut a notch in each piece of steel the right size and shape to fit over a bolt. The result was ugly, rusted, crude *somethings* that vaguely resembled the kind of straight- or curved-handle wrenches sold in stores.

These ugly, crude things worked—once we fit the notch over the bolt, we could grab the other end of the tube or pipe with a gloved hand, twist and ratchet the contraption in whatever direction was needed to loosen the bolt, and remove the bolt. Each person on the crew would go to work with one of these things and do the job we needed to do, using tools that no one would give to his worst enemy.

This make-it-yourself, jury-rigged, incredibly practical, notched-pipe tool amazed me when I first worked at the plant. Of course, from growing up on a rural farm, I knew about the kind of tools that farmers made themselves to save hard-earned money, but I also knew about the fancy tools that came from hardware and farm-supply stores. Those had brand names printed or engraved on the side and were made smooth, curved, and shiny, usually with a textured surface that increased your grip. The notched-pipe tools we used at the plant literally were pieces of junk. If they worked, why would anyone spend good money to buy sleek-looking, brand-name tools?

I was only eighteen, but from that lesson using the plant mechanic's handcrafted, junk-parts, notched pipe as a wrench, I understood what a tool should be. It should function in such a way as to perform the needed task. Nowhere should a tool's appearance come into play. The shiny surfaces don't need to be shiny, the textured surfaces don't need an exact and uniform texture, and nothing needs to be printed or engraved on the side. As long as I have a piece of strong pipe that has a notch cut in it the same size as the bolt, I can have a functioning wrench.

I learned that

A tool only needs to be good in the essential attribute that gets the job done.

"Good Enough" Tools

The lesson about handcrafted wrenches has stayed with me through the years. I have seen many other tools that possess no greater value than being able to do one job really well. I call these "good enough" tools.

Often, good-enough tools are simple things. A plastic spoon to use when eating chili in the cafeteria at work is a good-enough tool for me. It is not made of Sterling silver or silver plate or stainless steel, so it may break while I'm eating. If it does, I'll have to walk across the cafeteria to fetch another cheap, plastic spoon, but it gets the job done. It isn't a work of art with some classic-pattern initials scrolling on the handle, but it has the one attribute that is important—it does the job of a spoon, holding juices and solids long enough for me to transport them from bowl to mouth.

Whenever I eat chili, I can't help but think back to one time in college when my roommate brought take-out from our favorite Mexican restaurant back to our room. I was starving and the chili smelled sensational, but he'd forgotten to bring spoons for the chili. So, we improvised—we made spoons out of the lid of the container the chili came in. That lid made a very poor utensil, but it worked.

Processes can also be good-enough tools. One example is the stand-up meeting in which people meet—somewhere—to talk about the business and their immediate concerns, and then they disperse.

The stand-up meeting has few of the attributes of a classic meeting. There is no well-decorated meeting room, no hardwood table and comfortable chairs, no white board and projectors to illustrate the points made during the discussion, no fruit plate and beverage tray. People speak quickly and discuss only the most important matters, focusing effectively on the point. They communicate necessary information in a short period, with communication the goal of meeting. The stand-up meeting works extremely well because quality in communication is its important attribute.

We even had stand-up meetings at the asphalt plant. My dad would call his crew together for five or ten minutes before we started doing a job that was out of the ordinary. We didn't have a formal meeting room, so we met wherever we all would be working to do the day's job.

These meetings lasted just long enough for us to hear the necessary information about what was different about the assignment and how we were to do the work, and then we went to work. In my years as an engineer, I have been witness to too-few stand-up meetings. The one-hour-minimum meeting is the norm, even when the meeting topic only merits stand-up treatment. I miss those quick, effective meetings we had at the plant and suspect that the breakfast latte and pastries, posh surroundings, highly polished conference table, and comfortable chairs appeal more to our egos as engineers than to our sense of the best way for engineers to communicate.

People themselves can be good-enough tools. If that statement seems disrespectful, please let me clarify what I mean by this—I really don't think of people as "tools" that we use and then discard when we are done with them. But people are tools—in the sense that we employ them (unlike wrenches and folding knives, we cannot purchase them, but we do purchase their services through the wages we pay them), we give them things to do (as enlightening and interesting tasks as possible in the context of their performance of the job), and we try to see that they are well suited to the tasks we set for them. Although I do not contemplate whether such tools as wrenches and folding knives enjoy doing their jobs, I do want job satisfaction to be a factor to attract people to do the jobs I have for them. After all, I'm a people, too.

MR. PRACTICAL

I possibly could go on forever about the good-enough tools I use regularly. Given the abundance and effectiveness of such tools, it is hard for me to imagine that anyone would use anything else. I am Mr. Practical in this regard and wonder why anyone else would be different. After all, I never seem to use anything but good-enough tools—or do I?

Well, I *do* seem to use what I think of as "too much" tools. These are tools whose quality is valued in the context of many unimportant attributes. For example, the wristwatch or clock you consult to learn the time probably is a too-much tool. Most wristwatches are designed to be pieces of jewelry; most clocks are housed in cabinets built as pieces of furniture. Expensive, luxurious materials (diamonds and emeralds on the face of the watch, for example) that aren't essential to function and decorative elements (cartoon-character hands or cogs upon cogs come to mind) that obscure a clock face make far-too-many timepieces too-much tools.

Back in the late 1970s, as I recall the story, the good folks at Texas Instruments analyzed the economics of mass-producing a digital watch. They calculated how much it would cost to build a custom electronic circuit that would power the watch. They amortized the cost of the circuit over the number of units they would produce. They surveyed the market to determine overall market demand for wristwatches and how much they could charge for their watch.

The numbers looked good—very, very good—so they proceeded with The Great Digital Watch Project. They did everything as planned, put their watches on the market (I bought one), and they failed miserably. Why? The TI watch was functionally a success but commercially a failure because it was decidedly unattractive in looks. The folks at TI had not appreciated the fact that most consumers buy a watch to be jewelry, first, and a device to keep track of time, second.

Another example of a too-much tool is the automobile. A bit of history (according to me): The automobile was invented to transport people and things from one place to another. The important attributes of such a machine include speed, economy, carrying capacity, reliability, and safety.

The attributes automakers stress in their advertising include style, color, comfort, entertainment, sex appeal, and status. A CD player, satellite radio, and television have nothing to do with transporting people and things. They are, however, important attributes in selling too-much automobiles.

I often see the "too much" in process in the workplace. I've described the good-enough, stand-up meeting as the model of the good-enough tool, perfect for getting the job done efficiently and effectively. The weekly status meeting is just the opposite—another model of the too-much tool.

Weekly status meetings should be vehicles through which people receive information that applies specifically to their work. When everyone attends, the only information that should be discussed is that which applies to everyone. What happens, however, is that each person who has something to discuss seems to carry on a one-on-one conversation with the boss. Each individual's conversation takes place in front of everyone else, but has no relevance to anyone else. Weekly status meeting etiquette requires that all present appear to listen intently, whereas, in reality, for the majority of attendees, 99 percent of the time is, to put it bluntly, *wasted*—and waste is costly in more aspects than just time.

"WASTE NOT, WANT NOT" IS NEVER ANY FUN

There are many good-enough tools available to everyone, but too-much tools nevertheless find their way into most people's personal and professional lives, insinuating excess and waste into the most-carefully-made plans. It is tempting to think that we all would do well to eliminate the excess of too-much tools and use good-enough tools in their stead, but excess can have its place. The tale of the Buck folding knife illustrated, I hope, how something nonessential to knife function (the knife pouch) can be essential to a tool's being accessed in surprising ways. The pouch was nonessential to knife function, but it was essential to having that knife available for use in order to save a man's fingers.

Excess also has its place when it makes something *fun* as well as functional. I've reported that the primary purpose of the automobile is transport, but the automobile can also be a source of fun. The bells and whistles of CD players, satellite radios, and passenger-view televisions allow people to enjoy music, comfort, and the envy of friends and strangers while traveling from one place to another.

The value in enjoying excess—in moderation!—applies to process even when it's a "too-much" tool. I'm a guy and, like most guys, I like gadgets. I personally like the experience of walking through electronics and hardware stores, whether or not I actually make a purchase. As I walk about, I learn what items are new on the market, how people are using old things in new and innovative ways, and how these things might bring enjoyment to my life. Gals, on the other hand, love shopping, especially *shopping with friends*. Everybody acknowledges this, but I believe that what females *really* love about going shopping is just being together with their friends. They just happen to be walking through places that sell things while they are with their friends.

Weekly status meetings generally are too-much tools—and a bore—but these meetings, like shopping, provide a time for people to be together and chat. A large part of what is enjoyable about meetings has nothing to do with work *per se*. Joking, laughing, and enjoying the company of others are good things to do in the workplace. People who help make everyone they work with happier, better workers and who bring out the best in everyone else are good-enough tools.

Unlike some managers I've known over the years, I don't think that fun is a waste of resources. Work should be pleasant as well as productive, and I think the two go together. In my experience, people who enjoy their work tend both to accomplish more and to build better-quality products.

FINDING WHAT'S IMPORTANT

The good-enough tools that I have employed in the years since I first used handmade wrenches at the plant have great value to me. I follow three steps for finding such tools:

1. I identify a specific brand-name tool that has the desired functionality.
2. I list the important attributes of the tool.
3. I brainstorm to identify all possible items that possess those attributes.

The process begins with a simple question: "What do I want?"

I try to answer this question by naming one specific tool or process. If I want, say, a timepiece, I could answer, "I want a gold watch." From this answer, I determine the qualities that I deem important.

My next question is, *"What are the important attributes of the thing I want?"*

To answer, I make a list of the attributes of the specific item. For the timepiece, I'd list such attributes as gold, handsome, heavy, portable, and keeps track of time.

For each attribute in the list I ask, *"Do I need this attribute?"*

For example, "Do I need gold?" "Do I need portable?" I continue questioning, citing each attribute in the list in order to reduce the list to essential attributes.

My fourth question is, *"What can I use?"*

I review the short list of essential attributes and try to find other tools that possess them. If I find an item that possesses the essential attributes and is simple and inexpensive, I may have identified a good-enough tool. Continuing with the example of the timepiece, assume that my list of important attributes only contains "portable" and "keeps time." *Aha!* A one-dollar Texas Instruments surplus plastic watch is a good-enough tool.

Now let's take a process example. Suppose I want to create the outline for a book. My first question, "What do I want?" evokes my response, "a word processor that has an outline feature." I have seen people use this feature, so I know how it works. Of course, to make the best use of a word processor, I will also want a computer with a big screen (my eyes are not as strong as they used to be), a flat surface on which to place the computer, and a reliable source of electricity. The word processor does the job, but other items and tools will make it work better for me.

What is the important attribute of the thing I want? A word processor has process attributes as follows: It can be used for text entry, to display text, to store text, and to move text. Which of these attributes are important to me? Well, in this case, all four attributes I listed are important.

Finally, I ask, "What can I use?" My first response to this question is that I can perform three of the four tasks that I've listed as process attributes simply by jotting words in ink on paper. However, I cannot move text around on a page without a lot of crossing out and rewriting, so paper may not be a good-enough tool. I need to think of something better. *Aha!* A pad of sticky notes and a wall possess all four attributes. I can enter, display, and store text using the sticky notes by writing on them and sticking them to the wall. Since they are sticky and not glued, I can move the notes around on the wall. Problem resolved, then. The sticky notes and the wall will be an inexpensive, good-enough process tool for creating a book outline. In fact, the solution is one I have made use of to outline a dozen or so long documents I have written at work as well as a couple of books I have written at home.

Thoughts on Making Wrenches

The handmade wrenches we used at the asphalt plant worked well. The same is true for plastic spoons and stand-up meetings. These good-enough tools possess the essential attributes to do a job, but little else.

Managers should look for and use good-enough tools. Seeing value in raw materials is all-important in all economies. The dot-coms of the 1990s consumed resources through excessive bonuses, benefits, and wasteful expenses. When the dot.com companies failed, people lost jobs and families suffered. Maybe these companies would have been victims of the overall economy. Perhaps they would have failed anyway even if they had been conservative in their spending, but maybe not.

My personality and upbringing push me toward frugality and efficiency, but, as I have noted above, I also believe in having fun at work. The words "fun," "frugality," and "efficiency" are likely to mean different things to different people, stirring people to argue about which way their actions lean. But that's okay with me because I also believe in choice. I personally feel it is best to conserve resources by using good-enough tools, and I prefer to spend these conserved resources on the things and at the time I choose.

CONCLUSIONS

As I think back on my job crushing rocks, shoveling rocks, and watching rocks flow by, I marvel at the many productive ways mankind throughout the centuries has used rocks. Rocks, of course, can have a negative effect—I wince at the thought of dirty, little, pointy-surfaced objects that slip into my shoe, causing me to limp in pain. And I'm certainly not a happy camper when rocks push up through the soil in my backyard as if a bumper crop, damaging the blades of my lawn mower or slicing a gash in my shin as contact with the mower blade sends them flying.

Rocks can be pesky nuisances, but most often, they are to be valued, literally forming foundations for our homes, roads, and buildings. Rocks, rusty metal pieces, shiny knives, and myriad other objects are the raw materials with which we structure our lives. Some are obviously useful, while others take some thought to put to work. I believe that the more thought people give to ways to creatively and effectively use resources found around them, the more the workplace will benefit.

The lessons I've learned about raw materials and good-enough tools bear repeating:

Stuff that is lying around can be quite useful.

The most important use of a tool may be the least expected.

A tool only needs to be good in the essential attribute that gets the job done.

REFERENCES

[DEM03]   T. DeMarco and T. Lister, *Waltzing With Bears: Managing Risk on Software Projects* (New York: Dorset House Publishing, 2003).

[PHIWEB]   See www.iccknives.com.

THREE

Integrity

I am always looking for ways to help my group perform better. One characteristic I have noticed that helps improve group performance overall is the *integrity of individuals* within the group. That observation may not seem earthshaking, but the assets I've uncovered as the result of understanding the degree of each individual's integrity have been significant.

Every person in the group should be viewed from multiple perspectives, not just from the one dimension that corresponds directly to the job he or she performs. If all we, as managers, see is a flat representation of each person, we won't know about—and therefore will not be able to put to good use—the complete (professional and personal) facets of the person. Seeing a person from different perspectives—say, by appreciating someone as the concert-level pianist, Rubik's Cube regional champion, and Cub Scout troop leader that he or she is *in addition* to being the group's star programmer—allows me to see a whole, multidimensional individual. Seeing the dimensions of a person gives me a better handle on that person's integrity, particularly in terms of his or her propensity toward a professional standard of behavior and soundness of judgment.

For me, observing people is easier when I take on the difficult task of standing still. I find that I can more completely appraise the actions and work of others when I just stand still and watch what is going on around me. The problem is, while standing still, I appear to be doing nothing—and I hate doing nothing. As manager, I am supposed to show evidence of all the amazing abilities that propelled me to my lofty managerial position. Balderdash— that is *ego* talking, not integrity. Managers need to be still sometimes in order to give people space and time in which to do their job. Hard as it may be for me to resist the urge to intervene, by standing still, I show confidence in my staff and garner goodwill.

Integrity in the workplace manifests itself in a multitude of ways, but the three indicators I take particular note of are *choice, fear,* and *respect.* Here's my reasoning: We employ adults; adults usually make good choices; good choices make tasks at work flow better. The end result, if all goes as expected, is a more efficient and productive environment. Making the right choice, or even a reasonable and fair choice, is not likely to occur if an atmosphere of fear hangs over people. In my experience, when a manager shows respect for and confidence in his or her staff, fear dissipates, enabling workers to perform better and—dare I suggest—perhaps even to improve the quality of their personal lives.

Although I've rarely seen integrity discussed in the literature as a major factor in the workplace, integrity enables trust. Trust frees energy that can be directed at work. Instead of guarding their backsides and covering their tracks, people who work in an environment in which trust is present are free to perform many small acts that enhance everyone's effectiveness. The first thing we, as managers, have to do to make our domain a better place to work is to demonstrate our own integrity—and recognize integrity in those we manage.

WORKING WITH MY DAD

As I've mentioned, I worked with my father some of the time at the asphalt plant. Dad was a crew foreman, and although I worked with a couple of other crews from time to time, I mostly worked on his crew. Working in this mode felt uncomfortable at first. For one thing, I felt that I landed the job unfairly. It was obvious to everyone that I didn't win my job over other applicants during an open call for workers. I don't know what my father did to convince Louisiana Paving Company to hire me—all I know is that he landed the job for me and ensured that it was waiting for me between semesters. I didn't feel so conspicuous once I learned to do the job well because it was clear to all that I wasn't coasting in some easy position and I certainly wasn't in a cushy, no-show job.

A second factor that made me squirm a bit when I started at the plant was that I felt as if Dad were watching me. I felt I needed to behave better and perform better than anyone else working there. Whether he was watching me or not, I tried to live up to what I suspected were his expectations, and that made me work pretty darned near to perfection (or so I imagined). Thinking about it in retrospect, I guess the plant got what it paid for—and more—and I really shouldn't feel a twinge of guilt, but I still do, even to this day.

Working with Dad allowed me to suffer some fairly regular angst, but it also provided me with an incredible opportunity few sons get to experience. I got answers to the difficult question, "Who is this man?"

At home with my mother and brothers and me, he was "my dad," the smartest and wisest person in the household (at least my mother let us think that). At the asphalt plant, however, I wasn't sure how well Dad measured up. The field was broader, and there were people around who also were smart and capable. I'm embarrassed now that I fretted this way, but I was young, without experience in the working world, and I worried how Dad compared to all these other people. I wondered what other adults thought of him. What I didn't anticipate was what the answers to those questions would mean to me in time.

Seeing how my father was respected and how he interacted with people at the plant taught me a great deal about working with people, but the big lesson I learned from seeing my father at work was the following:

I can learn much about a person by seeing him or her in a different setting.

WITNESSING INTEGRITY

At the asphalt plant, aspects of Dad's character and integrity that I never noticed at home were revealed to me. Observing him in a different place allowed me to see the many dimensions of this person named Neal Phillips. At work, he interacted with a conglomerate of rough-and-tumble construction workers. How rough the men were hit me during the first minutes of my first day. Dad had parked our car and walked with me to the trailer housing the plant office. It was customary for a new man (me!) to meet the district supervisor and a couple of other company men there on Day One on the job. I sat among these men in the trailer while they discussed the coming day's work. Foremen came and went, grabbing cups of coffee and exchanging patter.

What I noticed most this first day was that these men peppered their remarks with foul language and off-color jokes, the likes of which I'd never heard at home or at family gatherings. True, I had heard plenty of four-letter words and tasteless jokes back in high school and at more than one gathering at college, but I had never been in my father's presence while such language was uttered. The look on my father's face showed his discomfort at being in a room with me, hearing this low-life talk.

Or so I thought at the time. In retrospect, I think Dad was not so much embarrassed for either of us as he was disappointed in the men in the trailer. They were behaving in a way that he considered damaging both to themselves as well as to the younger men who worked on their crews.

From this initial impression, I believed that these men were a breed apart from the adults I had been around to that point in my life—dramatically different in every way from my safety zone of relatives, friends, shopkeepers, doctors, and teachers. The language the men at the plant used, the clothes they wore, the way they threw tools about and slammed doors on the heavy equipment—everything about them struck me as coarse and loud, and decidedly off-putting. With time, however, I learned that, although different from the people I had grown up knowing, these men were kind, helpful, and trustworthy. I saw firsthand how generous they were with their time and working-world knowledge as they helped turn a naïve and sheltered young man into a multidimensional adult with developing integrity and character.

My father's integrity was something I had assumed I understood until I worked with him at the plant. There, I saw that his behavior at work matched his behavior at home. Two different situations, and I expected him to behave two different ways, because that is what I had been doing to that point in my life. The way I behaved at school with my friends was not the way I acted at home. Here, however, was my father acting the same in two different situations. Working on his crew, I saw him from another perspective—foreman, mentor, supervisor, boss, teacher to his men—but he behaved the same way he behaved with our family and friends. My eyes began to open.

I learned something more about Dad's integrity after he died in 1990 as the result of an automobile accident. My mother was selecting pallbearers for his funeral and wanted to include men from the plant. I made a couple of suggestions before learning that there was one man that she would not choose: a supervisor who had once instructed my father to misrepresent the facts on a form that had to be submitted to the State of Louisiana. My father had refused to do so—at the risk of losing his job. What struck me in my mother's story was not Dad's refusal to lie (Dad did *not ever* lie), but that he was made physically ill by the instruction. It upset him greatly that the supervisor would ask him to do something that his behavior—the core of his integrity—had for years on the job demonstrated he would not do.

I don't think Dad was perfect. He had his faults, as we all do, but duplicity was not one of them. He didn't change his demeanor or speech to fit the situation at hand. I think there were times in life when this hurt him, but he nevertheless always chose long-term integrity—with its consequences—over situational ethics and temporary gain.

Managing With Multiple Views

People are not only what they seem to be when on the job. As a manager, I work with many of the same people every day. Sometimes I think I know my colleagues well, but there are many sides to each and every person, and in the workplace, I may only see one dimension. If I know about their other dimensions, I may be better able to manage our work.

I have had a multidimensional view of only a few dozen people in my life. Those rare instances of seeing multiple sides of people who were not in my immediate circle of family and friends made a deep impression on me. One such person was Administrative Manager at the American Embassy in Lagos, Nigeria.

Her name was Betty, and some people referred to her as "Betty, the Communicator-Hater," or "Betty, the Screaming Terror." She yelled a lot at work, especially at the Communicators, whose job it was to operate equipment that allowed Embassy personnel to communicate with their counterparts in government back in the United States. She yelled at many other people, too. Once when I was in her office discussing an issue concerning a worker's passport, she stopped our conversation several times to yell out to staff members working in outer offices. She didn't call these people in to speak with them; she just yelled orders from her desk. I guess they heard her and knew what to do.

There was another side to Betty, however, which was revealed to me one day when she approached me in an Embassy hallway to ask about weekend church services she knew I attended. She explained that she wanted to attend services but was worried that the time involved would not fit with her regular weekend activities. I immediately assumed those activities included sleeping late and going to the beach because that's how most Americans in Lagos spent their free time. But, as Betty continued speaking, I was shocked to learn that she spent most of every weekend holding and caring for abandoned babies at a nearby orphanage.

I had not yet visited a Nigerian orphanage but several friends had described the stark horror and hopelessness. I stood dumbfounded for a few moments in the hall while I absorbed the incongruity and struggled with the fact that one small glance from a different place had turned a flat caricature into a full-bodied, multidimensional person. Here was Betty—the person who made life at work miserable for many people, the most avoided person in the community—describing weekends devoted to giving love and human contact to orphaned babies so that they might grow up having half a chance at normal lives.

The concept that feelings (the dimension of Betty I had neglected to consider) affect actions is fairly mundane, but I often forget that the concept applies as much at work as at home. I have seen other managers do the same, seeming to want people to be robotic and do as they say, regardless of all else. I am thankful that, on most days, I can see the folly of allowing the flat-world view to rule my actions.

HONORING PEOPLE

People do not exist in a flat world. If I am managing work well, I understand this and act accordingly. One thing I try to do is honor them. The simplest way I know to honor people is to use "appreciations" *(see detailed discussions on this topic in* [SAT88], [SATI88], *and* [KAR02]).

In an appreciation, I might say something like, "Roy, I appreciate how you always show up on time and always tell me the facts. Thank you." I say this directly to Roy, sometimes in private and sometimes in front of colleagues.

A key to giving appreciation is to be specific about both the person and the deed. This requires *thinking before speaking.* Often, someone who wants to appreciate the efforts of another falls down when saying the words. For example, too many people stand in front of a group and say, "I would like to thank everyone for their work on the turnaround project."

The speaker's first mistake is using the words "I would like to thank . . ." The person who utters those words is not thanking anyone, but rather is expressing his or her *desire to thank* someone. The crowd is left waiting for the thanks. Of course, everyone really understands what the speaker means, but saying "I would like" is a weak way to convey appreciation. Be direct: Thank people.

The second problem is that the person is thanking *"everyone."* I am not "everyone" and neither is anyone else. I am an individual and want recognition for myself when I have earned it. Thanking "everyone" is vague and lacks sincerity. Thank specific people *by name.*

The third problem is that the speaker is thanking people for "their work on the turnaround project" without seeming to know what any one person actually did. If one person did something special, thank that person by name for the specific job that he or she did.

The second and third problems point to the fourth: The speaker has not spent any resources on this appreciation. He or she has not spent time, energy, or emotion to learn either the names or the specific contributions of the individuals. As managers, we should spend time, energy, and emotion to appreciate and honor people. I include emotion in this list because some people become emotional during an appreciation. Many will want to hug one another, and some will cry. I am uncomfortable with even this minimal level of emotional display at work, but ironically, my discomfort is my greatest resource. People know that I am uncomfortable, so when they see me experiencing embarrassment with each individual who shows emotion, they realize how sincere I am about offering the appreciation. They see that I truly care about honoring the chosen individuals.

I noted earlier that appreciations are the simplest way I know to honor people, but they are difficult to do correctly. When I first learned about appreciations, I felt that they were *impractical*, taking too much time, and *inappropriate*, breaking down formality and encroaching upon the dignity of the workplace. I would shudder when I needed to look directly at someone to tell him or her that I appreciated both the person and the deed. I was not taught that kind of direct interaction at home, in engineering school, or at the asphalt plant, and I've certainly never seen it done with any regularity by others in my more than twenty years of working as an engineer.

After practice (sometimes face-to-face with a family member or friend, sometimes in front of a mirror to get myself comfortable with looking directly at a face), I found that appreciating others became easier. More importantly, letting others know you appreciate them often has beneficial results. First, people who are honored tend to perform thereafter at a higher standard, showing that they are worthy of honor. Second, whether I give my appreciation in person, in writing, or both, in almost all cases, people come to me and thank me for my appreciation.

PRACTICING INTEGRITY

I strive to practice integrity daily. To me, this means behaving according to the same principles at work, home, and everywhere else. It means conducting myself in the same manner at all times and in all situations. Such consistency isn't easy to achieve—it requires resolve, discipline, and energy.

One area where I struggle to practice integrity is in the office. Staying true to my personal and professional principles and standards in my dealings on the job with both superiors and subordinates can be difficult at times. I want *and need* people who work on the projects I manage to tell me the true picture in terms of deliverables, schedule, cost overruns, and the like. If I don't have the full picture of what is happening on the project, I cannot manage effectively.

Just as I must get the truth from those I manage, I also must provide the truth to my own management. When I report project status to my managers, I know they really don't want to hear bad news. So, if bad news must be communicated, I may experience a twinge of temptation to betray my integrity and "spin" the truth a bit, but I do not—for numerous reasons, only one of which is that people I manage will see and hear me talking to my managers and will know if I don't tell the complete truth. The consequence of this is not good: If my people witness my failure to stay true to my own integrity, they may feel they have license to follow my example instead of my words, imitating my lapses.

Another test of integrity on the job can come when someone agrees to be an intermediary between colleagues. For example, suppose Joe tells me that Bill's work is not up to our standards. I agree with Joe and commit to telling Bill. Bill, however, is a hardworker who always tries to please, and I don't want to crush him by telling him that we are unhappy with his work. In theory, I should tell Bill the bad news, but I cannot seem to deliver the message. In meeting with Joe, I agree with him, but when facing Bill, I am swayed by his good intentions and, by not telling him the truth, appear to agree with him. By my duplicitous behavior, I betray my integrity. Of course, if I am the manager of one or both of these men, my response to Joe's message must be governed by whatever I deem is best for the project. If Joe is correct and the work of the project suffers because Bill's performance is poor, I must talk truthfully with Bill, document the discussion for Bill and for the Personnel and Human Resources departments, as applicable, and give Bill a probationary period within which to improve.

The best way I've found for handling one person's criticism of the work done by a colleague or teammate is to avoid getting in the middle. If Person A needs to pass information to Person B, he or she should pass it directly, not through a go-between. In the scenario described above, there may be more going on than would first appear. For example, perhaps Joe cannot tell Bill directly because Joe is failing the integrity test. By this I mean that possibly Joe acts one way when Bill is not present (telling me the truth about his dissatisfaction with Bill's work and getting me to agree to tell Bill) and acts another way when Bill is present (by not telling Bill the truth about the quality of his work, he gives Bill the incorrect impression that his work is satisfactory).

As a third party, I can best help Joe behave congruently and according to his convictions not by being a go-between, but by facilitating a conversation in which Joe can explain to Bill what improvement is needed (*for more on congruent behavior, see* [WEI94]).

Thoughts on Working With My Dad

I treasure my memories of the years I worked with my father. Those years gave me many opportunities to see him through the eyes of others. From the experience, I learned that he was thought highly of as a fair-minded and compassionate boss, an honest and reliable employee, and an intelligent and dependable colleague.

In a way, I also got to see myself through the eyes of others while working at the plant because the people with whom Dad worked clearly valued what he had taught his son at home. Knowing this helped me to become a better worker at the plant and a more appreciative member of my family. It was at that point that I learned that I need multiple views before I can even come close to understanding another person and how best to work with him or her.

FLAGGING TRAFFIC

During my first few weeks with Louisiana Paving, I worked on a road crew. The first week, we prepared a section of two-lane highway for overlaying with new asphalt. The second week, we did the paving.

To overlay a two-lane road, the crew would work on one lane and allow traffic to pass on the other. As the newest member of the crew, I was assigned to one of two flagman jobs. I stood at one end of the paving site and stopped traffic while the flagman at the other end directed traffic to proceed toward me over the open lane. When he stopped the traffic on his end and signaled to me to start mine up, I would then give my side of traffic the okay to use the open lane.

Flagging traffic for Louisiana Paving meant I had to stand on the road for eight hours straight without a significant break. I could not take a break to sit; I could not take a break to eat lunch; I could not take a break for anything other than one or two quick bathroom breaks. Standing out there in the suffocating summer air and breathing in fumes from hot asphalt and idling motors, I would day-dream about just about everything. The happiest moment in my day came around noon when someone would bring my lunch box to me so that I could try to eat. I emphasize the word "try" because it is not easy to unlatch a lunch box one-handed, shake a sandwich out of waxed paper, and eat while the other hand holds the flag and waves the traffic through.

Eight hours is a long shift and, despite my day-dreaming to get my mind on matters other than traffic flow, I was bored silly. Flagging traffic requires just enough mental exertion to prevent a person from doing anything that benefits the brain, but it does not require enough mental exertion to keep a person interested. Flagging traffic is one of those in-between activities that numbs the mind and exhausts the body. After standing on a road for eight hours, everything hurt. My feet hurt, my arms and legs ached, my back twinged, and, under my hard hat, my head felt ready to explode. Standing in one place on a Louisiana road in summer is downright miserable. Drinking iced coffee or ice water would have been nice, but all that liquid would have made me even more uncomfortable since bathroom breaks were limited.

Flagging traffic undoubtedly was the worst job on the road crew. Digging ditches, shoveling asphalt, picking up trash—these were all more desirable jobs. No wonder road crews always made the new guy flag traffic. Flagging traffic did, however, provide me with an important lesson:

Sometimes, the hardest thing to do is to just stand still.

THE LEAST WAS THE MOST

Thinking back on my long week of flagging traffic, I am struck by how common it is for managers to assign a most-important job to a least-important person. The job of flagman was given to the least-experienced people on the road crew because, I imagine, if a person couldn't flag traffic, he or she probably couldn't be trusted to do any job that required more brains or skill.

In spite of being the least-experienced workers on a road crew, traffic flagmen perform what arguably could be called the most-important job of anyone at the site. The safety of the public and of the road crew itself depends on the flagman stationed at each end of the work area, whose job it is to ensure that vehicles pass through the site without injuring anyone or damaging anything.

Keeping people safe at a road-construction site is no small feat as there are myriad potential hazards. For example, large pieces of machinery, such as graders, dump trucks, and steamrollers, are difficult to stop once put into motion. The equipment is noisy, making it nigh impossible for operators to hear oncoming cars, honking horns, or people shouting directions to them to stop their vehicle. It may seem an exaggeration, but I have heard it said that the American road is more dangerous a place than the center arena of a modern war—and I'm inclined to believe that statement is pretty near true.

I've noticed that this least/most dichotomy exists in many places in society. For example, we entrust schoolteachers with imparting knowledge to our children, but we don't pay them salaries commensurate with the importance of their work. We pay school-bus drivers lower salaries than teachers, but we expect these drivers to do their job without even the smallest of mistakes, transporting our children safely and on time every school day.

THE INTEGRITY FLAG

To me, staying true to my integrity means doing what I know is right regardless of the circumstances of pay, social standing, or the like. In the context of this definition, one of the greatest tests of integrity I ever had was flagging traffic. I was not paid much and I did not feel appreciated while I was flagging traffic—at least not by those drivers and passengers who were waiting impatiently in their vehicles. I could have worked with an attention commensurate with my pay, and possibly have allowed an accident to occur. Surely no one would blame the inexperienced and low-paid flagman, but despite my inexperience and low pay, I did the best job I could flagging traffic. I tried hard, paid attention, did not wander off for a break, and did not ask for the job site to shut down so I could eat lunch. The traffic flowed smoothly, and no one was injured.

In retrospect, I tried hard because of the people involved. First, of course, was the fact that my father had gotten me the job, and he trusted me to do it well, no matter the assignment. Second, there were the other men on the road crew. I had only just gotten to know them, but they were real people. I knew their names and their faces. I had learned something about their family lives, and I could not think of slacking off and allowing any of them to be in danger. Third, there were the people driving through the job site. I don't recall knowing any of them personally, but I could see their faces as they waited to pass. Some of them had children with them, and others were elderly, but all clearly were just people who were trying to proceed with their own lives. I realized almost as soon as I started the job that I couldn't allow myself to be responsible for anyone being hurt.

What I learned while standing on the road eight hours a day with a flag in my hand was that *people* are important above all, more important than seniority, level of pay, aching limbs, or job status. The advice I was given along with the flag on that first day was simply put: "Be careful or someone will get hurt."

In fact, however, I have seen people get hurt on the job in the years since I flagged traffic. Although the injuries did not occur on the road and were not physical, they were damaging nevertheless, crushing people's spirits and destroying their confidence. Often these injuries were caused by a lack of judgment, evidence of one person's lack of integrity. I saw, for example, what happened when someone decided that another person was not paying proper homage, and, to rectify this, he pounced on that other person with heavy words and biting tone. The damage was debilitating, and it could be likened to the damage someone might suffer in a car accident or on a job site, taking some victims weeks to recover, while others never really recover. While injured, these victims spread their pain among friends, family, and acquaintances.

It's All About People

The lessons that I learned from flagging traffic taught me about integrity and have led me to recognize the importance of people in all endeavors. There are two undeniable reasons for recognizing the importance of people. First, it is the right thing to do; second, it is the practical thing to do. Recognizing the role that people play is important to accomplishing work. We don't have a machine that will take an envelope across the street and give it to someone. We need a person to do this. We need people to answer other people's questions (unless they are merely FAQs to which automated responses can be scripted), to take the temperature of a sick child, and to write a computer program. People, not machines, do the real work in most all of our endeavors.

People work because of people. For example, I work primarily so that I will have the means to support my family and myself (although I do also work because I get satisfaction from doing the work itself). In addition to working to support themselves, people also work to support their hobbies or to pay, say, for education, entertainment, or travel. But in all of these instances, people are what really matter. There is a difference between working "because of" people and working "for" people. The concept of working *for people* strikes me as quite arrogant. It carries with it the idea that I am superior in some way to a person who works for me.

When I flagged traffic, I did the best job I could because of the other people nearby—I wanted them to be safe. I did not flag traffic *for* my supervisor. While I certainly sought his approval, it was not the reason I did my best.

Stand Still and Observe

One lesson I learned from flagging traffic was how difficult it is to stand still, observing others who are in motion while I appear to be doing little. There is something quite difficult about appearing to do nothing. Standing still so as to observe is especially difficult because most managers want to be in the mix. I, for example, want to do things for my own satisfaction, and sometimes, to show off a bit so that the younger guys know I can still do the job.

Another reason standing still and observing are difficult tasks for most managers is that doing so seems to be an admission that they do not know what is really happening. If a manager needs to stand still and watch, it must mean that there are holes in the systems the manager either has created or oversees.

In addition, a manager who is standing still and observing is paying attention to people instead of to *the job.* To this day, my field—engineering—is populated mostly by men, and there is the attitude at far too many job sites that "real men" do the work and leave the soft skills to someone else. The assumption is that if people provide status reports in black ink on white paper, that is all there is to it. Well, I have learned that that idea is a fantasy. I must stand still and observe if I really want to know what people think, what people are capable of, and what emotions they feel.

I believe that observing is one of the most important types of work a manager can do. It is by observing that I can learn what is happening in my organization. I learn what people are doing, how they feel, how a project is progressing, and ultimately, the quality of the product we are providing. One remarkable book that treats this subject remarkably well is *Quality Software Management: First Order Measurement*, by Jerry Weinberg (*see* [WEI93]). I highly recommend this book (the second volume in a four-volume series) to managers who are interested in learning how better to observe, as observing is its principal theme.

One responsibility of being a manager is to gather status reports to determine the health of both staff members and of the project. I can gather status updates via comparatively informal e-mail exchanges, by reading more formal status reports, and by talking to people. One very important factor to note is whether people are communicating to me what is really happening and how they really feel about it. I don't think people lie blatantly to managers like myself, but I have experienced occasions on which people did not express what they really were feeling.

Using Your Senses

When I was younger, I rarely told my supervisors how I felt. I did not have the confidence to tell my management, "I am worried. Even though we are on schedule now, I don't think we can keep this up. I think I may be making mistakes in the product, and those mistakes are slipping through our testing."

Instead, I said, "Things are looking pretty good."

My managers took my words literally and didn't observe me well enough to understand that I was not saying what I felt.

I try to use the five senses to observe what is really happening in the workplace. I first consider *sight*. I watch what people do while they talk. If they look at the floor and shuffle their feet (as I used to do) while telling me that things are pretty good, I stop and ask questions. "Why do you think they are pretty good?" "Can you give me two or three reasons why you think things are pretty good?" "Are there certain events that would have to occur for things to be *really* good?"

Assuming that you ask these questions and that you get answers that give you a more realistic picture of what is going on with the project, a final question to ask might be, "Is there something else you would like to tell me?" It also helps bring out facts instead of wishes when I tell the person of my own fears and how I used to answer "pretty good" when I was afraid to tell the truth.

Nervous habits tell the observer that all is not right in Projectland. For example, I would pace back and forth outside my boss's office when I wanted to tell him something that was difficult to admit. My manager usually noticed my apprehension and invited me to say what was on my mind.

The next sense to use is *hearing*. Listen to a person's voice when he or she reports project status to you. One indicator of trouble is when someone speaks without pausing or hesitating but halts suddenly when asked a question. I have heard numerous conversations between a manager and an employee that went like the following:

Manager: "How is the testing progressing?"
Tester: "Pretty good. I started yesterday and finished all the tests
we scheduled for the day."

> *Manager: "Good. Is the testing system functioning properly?"*
> *Tester: "Oh, yes. It is working better than ever before."*
> *Manager: "That's good to hear. How about Jane? Is she learning*
> *how to use the system?"*
> *Tester: "Jane, uh,"* (pause) *"yeah, Jane is helping me."*

The tester's pause, whether long or just a blip on the radar screen, should cause red lights to start flashing in the manager's head. There is something wrong with Jane and the test. Also, notice the second warning in the tester's last statement. The tester did not answer the question about Jane learning to use the system. This example seems obvious. How could anyone not notice the problem indicated by the tester's response? Well, I've missed such signals and observed others missing them as well.

Your sense of *smell* is another good detective. An observant manager can smell trouble on a project. When people spend long hours and weekends working in the office, the office smells like it. Excuse me if I am less than delicate here. When a person sits in a room fourteen hours a day, the room is likely to be permeated with body odor. Smelly food left in a trash can late Friday night has an odor at 7 A.M. on Monday morning that states more about the hours that people are working than any status report.

In the same manner, an observant manager can *taste* a troubled project. I like to drink coffee, and I can tell when the coffeemaker has been left on too many hours with coffee slow-boiling away. Such old coffee indicates that people have been working long nights and drinking coffee to stay awake. Stale pizza in the refrigerator is another indicator.

Gathering project information through *touch* is tricky but possible. I have a friend whose parents were strict about how much television he watched each day while he was growing up. He looked forward to his parents leaving the house for a few hours to do errands because he could watch television without their knowing—or so he thought. His parents would tell him not to watch TV while they were gone, but he turned on the set as soon as they drove away. He turned it off before they returned, but they always seemed to know that he had been watching. A few years later, he learned that one or the other would put a hand on the top of the set. A warm set meant that it had been on, and my friend's activity was known. Similarly, an observant manager can tell whether computers, testing tools, copiers, and other equipment have been in recent use by placing a hand on the equipment.

By focusing on even small changes, a manager can find truth, whether or not staff members provide accurate status reports. So, when someone changes tone of voice, cadence of speech, or how rapidly he or she is breathing, an important message is being sent. Pay attention to what the reasons behind a change in office odor or in the smell or taste of coffee might indicate. These changes just might indicate that an important message is lurking unspoken. To find out the message, stop what is happening and ask questions.

STANDING STILL WHILE I CHANGE

One of the greatest challenges a manager faces is associated with leading an organization through change. It is natural for a manager to want to steer people quickly through change in hopes of reaping the benefits of a new and better situation. Trying to institute change too quickly, however, rarely works out the way it is hoped. In most situations, the best thing to do is stand still, wait, and watch.

I find it helpful to have a model or blueprint for change, including both planned and possible change. A brilliant model is the Satir Change Model (*see* [SAT88], [SATI88], *and* [WEI97]). The Satir Change Model posits that the emotional reactions of the individuals directly influence how they handle change. The model is simple to understand and use. There are four states in the Satir Change Model, as follows: (1) Old Status Quo, (2) Chaos, (3) Integration and Practice, and (4) New Status Quo. When something changes in the workplace, the organization incorporates the change in the context of these four phases.

In the Old Status Quo state, work proceeds as expected. People can predict what will happen with a high degree of success. The trouble is, people need to work hard to keep the system in balance—even if an organization refuses change, the environment around it changes. The hard work in the Old Status Quo state is spent keeping the organization afloat. Nothing new is created, and there is no innovation, no growth, and little job satisfaction. Many people find themselves stuck in this situation.

The Old Status Quo state ends and the Chaos state begins when an unavoidable element is introduced into the environment. This change jars an organization hard enough so that people can no longer maintain the status quo. Although they try to hang on to the old and familiar, they generally will need to introduce new initiatives or stronger processes in an attempt to combat the change.

In Chaos, nothing proceeds as expected. Old procedures don't work, and people are dazed and confused. They accomplish things only by bypassing all policies, running around until they find someone they know, and doing work in the hallways. They continue to have other strange new ideas and constantly want to try them out.

Eventually, an idea rises above the Chaos state and brings new possibilities, ushering in the Integration and Practice state. In this state, someone finds a practical way to deal with the change, which brings people to feeling a sense of relief and understanding. Although the organization—and its work—is no longer stuck in total chaos and things seem to be working again, it is typical for people's emotions to swing back and forth in this state. The process they must use now to do their job is unfamiliar, and causes them to experience feelings of doubt and to lose confidence. Whether they express the idea that what they are experiencing is too good to be true and will come crashing down any day, it is likely that they are worried.

At this point, the New Status Quo state emerges. Things become predictable again, based on changed processes and standards. The system is in balance, except this time, people are not working extra hard just to maintain that balance. People feel good about process and progress now because they are accomplishing daily tasks and have time and energy to innovate.

Change requires time. People need time to work their way through the second and third stages: Chaos first—and then Integration and Practice. If a manager steps in and proclaims, "Here is the clarification for your confusion," he or she is only introducing another confusing change. That new change will plunge everyone into a new state of Chaos. The well-meaning manager has cost the organization time since the Chaos state must repeat itself.

People in an organization need to try out their own ideas and keep trying ideas until they find one that will be a transforming idea. Any idea forced upon them by a manager is likely to be rejected as a foreign element. The transforming idea, the one that ends the Chaos state, must come from the people themselves if it is to be embraced by them. The manager must stand still and let people try ideas out for change.

Making a cake is somewhat analogous to chaos in change. There are ten or so steps in making a cake. The cake doesn't resemble a cake until the last step is finished. During all the prior steps, the jumble of ingredients just looks like a mess. There is nothing a manager can do at, say, Step 6 to make the mess look like a cake.

Standing still and watching while people struggle through change is difficult for most managers to do, but it is a powerful tool.

Thoughts on Flagging Traffic

I'm not really sure how managers at the Louisiana Paving Company felt about putting new people on the road crew and assigning them the starting job of flagging traffic. Maybe flagging traffic was the least popular job on the road crew, and so the crew foreman gave that job to the newest person on the crew just because that person's preferences mattered least to the company at that particular point in time.

Or maybe the flagging job provided a kind of unspoken test: If a person had the integrity to do that job well, that person probably had sufficient integrity to work for the company in other, more popular—and more challenging—capacities.

Louisiana Paving probably did not pay anyone much in the way of salary, but I never heard of anyone who stole materials, fuel, or other items from the job site. Despite working conditions, I think that, for the most part, we enjoyed high morale and high morality. This required some degree of integrity to be present in the people the company kept on as employees.

With the benefit of hindsight, I believe that Louisiana Paving had a solid way to test each new employee's integrity. The fact that I passed the test gave me a level of confidence that has stayed with me these many years since.

WORDS IN BOOKS

During lunch break one day, I overheard some of the men carrying on a fairly tension-filled discussion about the merit of reading books. Several men were commenting on a coworker who often spent his lunch break off by himself reading a book.

The discussion ran its course, and the two people who had had the most to say left the group to go back to their work. Still present were a couple of men who had sat silently during the conversation, one of whom—a short, skinny, wiry man in his late sixties—we all called "Shorty." Shorty looked straight at the rest of us and, in a matter-of-fact tone, said, "I know what's in every one of those books in the library." He paused for a few seconds, and then finished his statement: "Words."

Shorty's deadpan comment broke the tension and gave everyone a chance to relax and smile before the group broke up to go back to work. But I kept thinking about what he had said. In one simple comment, he had covered two ends of the spectrum regarding mankind's reverence for the written word. First, he brought all authors to his own level by intimating that they were just human, like himself, and had no more and no less to work with than he had—just "words." Second, he implied that reading someone else's words was a waste of time because he already knew that there were just words in all those books in the library. He later explained to me that he had not read any "real" books in many years (at least fifty!) and commented that he really had no intention of reading even a single book in the foreseeable future.

His statement shocked me. I couldn't imagine going a month without reading a book, whether for my own pleasure or for my education, but I think I can understand why Shorty did not share my view. Although gainfully employed at the plant year-round, he was a self-educated Southerner of a certain age and bias, and he had been responsible for contributing to the support of an extended family since Grade Six. When he made his lunchroom statement, he had neither the will nor the inclination to waste so precious a commodity as "free" time reading words another man had written. To me, such behavior—avoiding reading—indicated a fear that reading for one's own pleasure or enlightenment was somehow sinful and wasteful—the opposite of what I consider it to be. So, although I am not entirely confident that I understand everything Shorty meant by his statement about books and words, what I have taken from it is the following:

Too much fear combined with too little respect and too little choice often go hand in hand.

FEAR AND RESPECT—AND CHOICE

Fear and respect often go together, but their relationship puzzles me. When I make a list of things I respect because I am somehow in awe of each thing's power, and a second list of things I fear, I do not have many entries that appear on both lists. For example, I had respect for the large machines that were used at the asphalt plant. Operators could manipulate them to move enormous amounts of material with ease, regardless of the harsh conditions. I did not, however, fear those monstrous machines. I understood how they worked and knew how to turn off each one of the machines with a flip of a switch in order to bring it to a harmless stop.

I do fear some things, but I generally don't also respect them. For example, I fear falling off the roof of my two-story house whenever I am up there cleaning gutters or doing repairs. I don't, however, think in terms of either respect or disrespect when I think of being up on the roof. Gravity is just a law of physics and, for whatever reasons, I don't think about it much.

Shorty, on the other hand, tied fear and respect together. He let us know that he had little respect for the written word. "Those books," as he called them, were full of words from just some other person. In one way, Shorty was right. A person who writes a book is just a person who writes a book, and he or she should expect to have no higher or lower standing in the scheme of things than any other person.

In another way, Shorty was wrong. A person who writes a book is not "just another person" for the simple reason that no one is "just another person." We each are unique and bring something special to this world. Some of us do things that are more easily recognized than others.

Shorty also expressed a fear of books. During my years in the engineering field, I have met a handful of people like Shorty who seemed to fear the written word. One was a gentleman who was undeniably accomplished in his area, but he would push back from the table when someone placed a written report in front of him, behaving as if the document were a poisonous snake.

My attitude toward books changed when I finished college, primarily because I could choose what books to read. Instead of having books pushed on me by teachers and other authority figures, I could decide for myself what to read, and as a result, I read constantly.

My love of books, while not unique, is not universal. I have met many educated professionals who do not read books. They generally do read professional journals and special-interest papers, in order to stay abreast of advances in their field, but they do not read books for the fun of it.

There is, however, a difference between Shorty and these other people. Adults in my profession sometimes do choose to not read books, but it is because they don't enjoy reading—it does not provide enjoyment, and so they do not read unless they can directly benefit as a professional. Shorty, on the other hand, avoided books because he was afraid of them; he acted in the absence of choice.

WORKING WITH AND THROUGH PEOPLE

The message I took from Shorty's words—a message that created in me a swirling mixture of fear, respect, and choice has come back to me many times during my career. From Shorty, I learned that people can be afraid at work. Shorty's fear of books helped me notice that there are people who avoid books because they fear that they'll be adversely influenced by another's thinking or because they fear that the time they take to read a book will be detrimental to other, more life-critical endeavors. Shorty's fear of books also helped me see that there are people who avoid books by choice. People at work choose what they do. Position, power, money— these things may affect fear and choice, but they don't determine them.

FEAR AT WORK

Shorty showed me that fear can affect how we do our work. I needed years to fully grasp this concept—fear is a common human emotion, and we humans spend so much of our time at work. I understood that uneducated and low-paid laborers at an asphalt plant might have their fears. They struggle economically each day and have reason to fear instability.

I didn't understand, however, how it could be that well-educated, highly paid professionals would have fears at work. I could not believe that someone would be afraid to stand up in front of a group of people and talk. I could do that, so what was the problem with someone who couldn't? The things that don't bring fear to me seem silly when they frighten other people.

Not everyone is this lucky. A colleague of mine named Dell fears confrontation. He works with outside contractors and has had many occasions when he needed to say things like, "You have not accomplished the work you planned. This is the sixth month in a row that you have not accomplished what you planned. We need to do something different here."

Dell, however, is afraid to say anything that might hurt the contractors' feelings. His fears ruin his job performance and allow the contractors to continue missing deadlines, wasting money, and failing to deliver products.

I wish Dell were the only person I have known on the job whose fears damage performance and hurt the organization. But this is a real and widespread problem.

RESPECT AT WORK

Shorty's comments on words in books have caused me much thought through the years. Books are full of words; I cannot argue with that. I've always respected the words in books—often too much. If some message were printed in a book, I generally gave it credibility without critical thought. I've always respected people who write books—often too much, as well. If a person has written a book—even one not published—I still tend to give great respect to that person.

Every person with whom I work is due respect. I believe this because every person at work is just that—a person, and at the very least, people deserve respect. The work, the product of a person's efforts, similarly is due respect. Products don't automatically appear simply because a person has shown up at work each day. Products are the result of some person's hard work and perseverance, both admirable qualities in any person.

Shorty's comments on words in books have been a puzzle that I haven't solved in thirty years. I respect him for that and for so many other attributes.

CHOICE AT WORK

Shorty was afraid of books. He didn't admit this in so many words, but I've come to believe that avoidance combined with disdain add up to fear. As I noted earlier, I've known other people who avoid books. They read articles and newspapers, perhaps, each day, and have good feelings for people who cherish books, but they choose to not read books. I consider those people to be healthy adults, even if I think they are mistaken in their choices.

As a manager, I want to work with healthy adults who like to make choices for themselves, and it seems that we all want this. That is, however, until I see these healthy adults making choices— for and by themselves—that disagree with my (managerial) instruction.

It has taken me years to comprehend that people do make choices for themselves at work. I knew this to some extent early in my professional life, but only recently have I been able to utilize that knowledge, seldom to better effect than in my dealings with a man I used to work with named Doug. He never seemed happy at work. He wore a scowl on his face and frequently—*and quickly*— turned that scowl to anger. People would urge me, "Don't pass that news to Doug because he'll get mad."

I finally decided that Doug, like any other adult, could and did make choices. If he reacted to news with anger, that was his choice. I could react to his anger in a way that I chose.

In the past, I worried that my actions would make someone angry or sad or feel some other negative emotion, and that it was wrong for me to bring suffering to another person. In order to prevent such suffering, I felt I needed to "see" inside other people to assess how my speech and actions would affect them. I felt as if I failed as a manager when I didn't have the magical vision required.

Understanding that adults make choices for themselves relieved me of this burden. Knowing that I don't have the power to choose the reactions and feelings another person will experience makes my life much easier. I now can choose what I do and let other adults choose what they do. It is liberating to give up the fantasy of power over other adults. When someone becomes angry in my presence, I can choose to take the blame for his or her anger or I can choose otherwise.

WORKING WITH ADULTS

Shorty taught me to work with adults. This would seem to be easy to accomplish—all I have to do is check everyone's birth certificate and eliminate people under the age of eighteen. Age, however, isn't a reliable measure of adulthood. I know this is the case as I am well over twenty-one but, even on a good day, I probably only behave as an adult should about 90 percent of the time. When I fail to behave as an adult, people around me seem to fail as well. When I behave as a mature and proper adult, people around me usually do, too.

DIVERSITY

The men at the asphalt plant were diverse in every way imaginable—age, education, skills, physical attributes. For example, Shorty had seen his sixtieth birthday, and then some, come and go; I was not yet twenty. Shorty, as well as a number of the other men, had not finished Grade Six; I would soon graduate from college. But the scale was not always tipped in one direction: Most of those men, although without much formal education, were skilled machinery operators who could place tons of material within an inch of where they wanted it. I was a laborer who was not entrusted with anything more powerful than a flag or a shovel. Diversity in age, education, language, and culture of the men at the asphalt plant helped make it a place that was rich with opportunities to learn.

Most of the jobs and projects I have worked on since my years at the plant have been staffed by groups of people divided into teams, each team consisting of people with diverse skills and interests. One of the worst jobs I ever held was terrible primarily because it lacked diversity. That job was at a signal-processing lab, and I worked there for four long years. One of the reasons the job was so unbearable was because the people who had worked there for many years made life difficult for new hires, who either were ethnically or socially different from the old-timers or were interested in trying anything different from the way things had always been done. The old-timers banished diversity and considered taking time to help a colleague with a task or even to be pleasant to someone else an outright travesty.

The dominant culture in the lab was akin to an operations center, and the old-timers acted as if seconds ticking on the clock meant lives were being lost. Taking time to think was considered wasteful and punishable, say, by the silent treatment or by harsh assignments requiring overtime during holiday seasons. Anyone who preferred to think quietly or who wanted to be pleasant to others was derided until he or she left for a happier environment. I managed to last four years, but, to this day, I question why I didn't leave sooner for the sake of my mental health.

I learned a valuable lesson during those four years, however, and I try always to apply it when hiring new staff members or putting a team together. The lesson I learned is that it is helpful to assess each person's personal style and temperament in order to build a diverse staff. It wasn't until some years later that I learned to use the Myers-Briggs Type Indicator (MBTI), which measures individual preferences (*see* [KEI84]), but even at this early point in my career, I was aware, for example, that I am quiet and reserved, and prefer to stay to myself when I am tired. In contrast, people with a different temperament from mine may seek the company of others in order to regain a higher level of energy.

Another preference of mine is to sit alone and plan each step in detail before starting an endeavor; others jump into activities without wishing to think ahead to the outcome. When I understand my own preferences as well as the preferences of others, I, as manager, can better prepare for different situations.

Although the following advice should be common sense, I offer it anyway: Do not staff a company, a department, a team, or even, dare I suggest, a life-partnership with people who are all of the same type. Identify people's preferences and choose for diversity. Pay attention to individual strengths and weaknesses, but especially to weaknesses, because when something happens that attacks one weakness, the entire unit will fail at the same time. Diversity in the components that make up a unit—whether consisting of two people or two hundred—provides resilience.

I learned even more about the importance of diversity during my first job out of college when my supervisor sent me with two other men on a two-month trip out of the country. Before we began our trip, our supervisor told us that he had selected the three of us for our differences. To help us understand how our differences were important, he pointed out that one of the other men was, like me, quiet and analytical, but that, unlike me, he had years of experience.

My supervisor explained that he picked me for the team because I was freshly schooled on a wide array of new technologies and methods, and he believed that I would bring to the team a willingness to introduce these new techniques, albeit well-thought-out and planned to the *nth* degree. He also explained that although my senior counterpart also preferred to survey a situation, think it through, and then take action, his action might not seem to make sense to me at first, but that it usually worked. He noted that the third member of our team might seem impulsive to us as his preference was to dive into situations headfirst, displaying an energy that usually helped pull him through even if he did not always dive in the right direction.

Our supervisor helped us understand how our differences would work in different situations, and how my cautious loner's approach and up-to-date methods would complement the other men's greater experience and opposite styles. He also helped us see how each of us could work in a way contrary to our preferences when circumstances called for us to do so.

FEAR NO EVIL

If fear exists in the workplace, it hurts performance. When I believe that people fear something in the workplace, I know that I, as manager, can't choose how they respond, but I can help create a situation in which they are less likely to choose fear.

I know this because of my own personal experience, having had the misfortune of working places where people usually chose fear. The signal-processing lab I described earlier was one of those places. I came to work in a state of fear almost every day. Having seen it happen to others at the lab, I was afraid that the old-timers would attack me as a person as well as attack my work, and that their attacks would cost me pay raises and any eventual promotions. Instead of doing what I knew was right, I reacted to my fear and tried to make the old-timers like me so that they would spare me—and my work. This was not a successful "plan."

Many other people came to work in a similar state of mind at the lab. I recall one day when several of us pulled a colleague, who had been our peer but now was several levels up in management, into a room and closed the door. We all had known and trusted one another for several years and were able to speak freely on subjects of concern for more than half an hour.

A knock on the door called our colleague away to another meeting, but before he left, he looked at us and, in a state of relief, said, "Whew. I haven't talked like that in a long time."

The sad fact was that the rest of us had not spoken freely for a long time either. We all worked in such a state of fear that we would not venture to tell people what we really thought. This hurt our ability to think and to solve problems and stifled the sharing of good ideas, causing us to spend our time executing tired ideas that would not rock the old-timers' boat. Looking back on this amazes me. I don't understand why I spent so many years living in fear.

In the lab, fear began as blame. Managers there concentrated on blaming other people whenever something went wrong. I quickly learned that something going wrong did not have any objective measure, but meant that one of the managers either did not like something or didn't like the person who did the something. These blame attacks conditioned us to believe that by *doing nothing*, we were likely to escape blame. Therefore, many of us concentrated either on doing nothing or on doing only what the managers had shown was approved.

As a manager, I strive to keep fear from creeping into the workplace. There are various ways to do this, one of the best being leading by example. I make mistakes—lots of them—so when I admit openly to these mistakes, I am telling others in the workplace that it is okay to make mistakes and that I understand that mistakes happen. Then I make it clear to them that I won't blame any person for making a mistake.

I learned much about driving out fear while working on a project during the late 1990s that my colleague Roy O'Bryan and I describe in *It Sounded Good When We Started* [OBR04]. I became involved with the project when it was about a year old, and I quickly noticed that whenever a problem surfaced, people spent much of their time explaining why the problem wasn't their fault. I thought that was curious as I hadn't said anything about fault, but fault avoidance was their primary concern.

With time, we were able to change this atmosphere of fear and blame into one of solving problems and moving forward. When someone told us of a problem, one of us would say something like, "Okay, I see that we have a problem. I am disappointed that it happened, and I can see from your expression that you are just as disappointed. What do you suggest we do about this?"

Notice that this approach contains nothing about who made this mistake. The underlying understanding is that we all make mistakes, so knowing the name of whoever made this one—and, by inference, whoever will make the next one—is not important. Also notice that this approach allows for the expression of emotion—that we are all disappointed—but doesn't get stuck there. It instead looks to the future and concentrates on what we—together—are going to do next.

Another approach to driving out fear comes from author and consultant Jerry Weinberg. In some of his workshops, Jerry suggests taking people through a series of "Then what would happen?" questions. For example, I mentioned earlier that I feared knocking on my supervisor's door and asking to talk with him. The fear-removing conversation would go something like the following:

Me: I am afraid to knock on my supervisor's door.
You: What would happen if you knocked on the door?
Me: My boss would tell me to go away.
You: Then what would happen?
Me: I would go away.
You: Then what would happen?
Me: I would come back later.
You: Then what would happen?
Me: The same thing might happen again.
You: Then what would happen?
Me: My boss would eventually ask me to come in and talk.
You: Then what would happen?
Me: We would talk.
You: Then what would happen?
Me: Things would be okay.

This conversation should help me see there isn't much to fear by knocking on my supervisor's door. A similar conversation could deal with a person's fear of admitting to a problem:

Me: I am afraid to tell the customer that we have a problem and will be late with the product.
You: What would happen if you told the customer that you have a problem and will be late with the product?
Me: The customer would get mad at me.
You: Then what would happen?
Me: I would feel bad about myself.
You: Then what would happen?
Me: I would go home sad.
You: Then what would happen?

and so on, down to the desired conclusion:

Me: I would deliver the product to the customer.
You: Then what would happen?
Me: I would start on the next project.

It has been my experience that while people may think they cannot eliminate their fear, they generally only need to do this "Then what would happen?" exercise once or twice to regain control of the situation.

BACK TO ADULTS

Shorty and the other men at the asphalt plant were all adults. For me, one of the joys of working at the plant was that these adults treated me as an adult, despite my obvious status as a college student working part-time. Because they treated me like an adult, I actually felt like an adult, and consequently tried my darnedest to act like one. The atmosphere provided me with another lead-by-example experience that I strive to follow to this day.

As manager, I strive to treat others as adults and I expect to be treated as an adult. One freedom that accompanies adulthood is freedom of choice. The adults who work with me may choose to be angry or sad as a reaction to something I do or say, and I let them be that way. Rather than criticizing their choice, I may question it or ask to understand it—but I don't attack it.

I also strive to avoid attacking another person's choice of reaction to a specific event. It is an attack when someone says something like the following: "You have no right to be angry! Stop crying! No one intended to hurt your feelings!" Instead of attacking, ask questions about someone's choices, such as: "You seem to be angry. What did you hear or see from me that led you to feel anger?" and "I see that you are upset. Would you like to discuss that with me?"

Adults should have equal value in this world, but they do not have equal ability. This is no great revelation, but I have forgotten this truth at times and become frustrated when some people in my charge have not done what I expected them to do. Coworkers and people I manage don't always know what I know and can't always do things I can do. My reaction to this disparity needs to be tempered by what is realistic given the circumstances; a show of my level of frustration does no one any good.

As a manager, I need to try to speak with adults on an adult-to-adult level. The attack statements I cited above ("You have no right to be angry!" "Stop crying! No one intended to hurt your feelings!") are examples of how adults sometimes speak to children. Another, even more destructive, example is, "You made a stupid mistake. You should be ashamed. Go to your room until I tell you that you can come out."

When the blaming shifts to child-to-child talk, the conversation is likely to digress to something along the following lines:

"You messed up again."
"Oh, yeah! Well, you messed up last week."
"Well, my mess-up is nothing compared to your mess-up. And you're smelly besides."

Adult-to-adult conversation should be structured so as to consider both the adults and the organization. For example, if I am one of the adults and I am speaking to an adult who reports to me but whose work has been problematic for my organization, I try to describe the problem and offer a solution that is in the best interest of all three parties. In a situation in which I've brought the problem to the attention of the other person and nothing has changed for the better, I might say, "John, we've talked previously about the fact that the choices you have made this past year have hurt everyone's efforts on this project. All our jobs depend on this project. Therefore, I see no alternative but to remove you from the project. I have asked Personnel to find you another job in the company."

In this brief discourse, I am speaking for myself as well as for the organization, telling John how I see things, placing the matter in context, and offering to help John find another job. I am neither blaming John ("You made stupid mistakes") nor making universal generalizations ("Everyone knows you mess up all the time"). There are undoubtedly better ways to handle every situation than the ways we sometimes use when we are under pressure or are not thinking at an adult level, but by practicing courtesy and dignity, we can make such encounters a win-win for all involved.

Thoughts on Words

I participated in or listened to many conversations while working at the asphalt plant. The discussions were memorable in part because I was young and the men at the plant were so much older than I, and in part because even the men without much formal education seemed so knowledgeable and wise in comparison to myself. The fact is, of course, that although I do remember the gist of many conversations, I don't remember many exact words. Shorty's comment about books is an exception. I can still hear his raspy, matter-of-fact voice as he spoke in that slow Southern drawl, and I believe I'll remember his exact words for as long as I live.

I don't know what happened to Shorty after my father passed away and my family's connection to the plant passed with him. I doubt that Shorty changed his mind and started reading books, but it is possible since, at the time, I had no intention of writing books, and I changed my mind. I'd like to think Shorty lost his fear and learned to choose to read, but there's no way to know.

What stays with me when I recall Shorty's words is that there is a strange relationship between fear and respect and choice. As a manager, I can use knowledge of how they relate to improve what goes on in the workplace. Fear exists within people, but it should not be the dominant catalyst at work. I would rather people be motivated by choice instead of by fear. One way to help choice replace fear is to reduce fear to tolerable levels. Once choice takes its rightful place, each adult should feel empowered to make his or her own choices. And once that happens, all I need to do is show that I respect each adult by acknowledging his or her choices.

CONCLUSIONS

I am fortunate that I experienced many lessons about integrity during my time with Louisiana Paving, with the following being primary:

I can learn much about a person by seeing him or her in a different setting.

Sometimes, the hardest thing to do is to just stand still.

Too much fear combined with too little respect and too little choice often go hand in hand.

REFERENCES

[KAR02]   N. Karten, *Communication Gaps and How to Close Them* (New York: Dorset House Publishing, 2002).

[KEI84]   D. Keirsey and M. Bates, *Please Understand Me: Character & Temperment Types,* 4th ed. (Del Mar, Calif.: Prometheus Nemesis Book Co., 1984).

[OBR04]   R. O'Bryan and D. Phillips, *It Sounded Good When We Started: A Project Manager's Guide to Working With People on Projects* (New York: IEEE Computer Society Press/John Wiley and Sons, 2004).

[SAT88]   V. Satir, *The New Peoplemaking* (Palo Alto, Calif.: Science and Behavior Books, 1988).

[SATI88]   V. Satir et al., *The Satir Model: Family Therapy and Beyond* (Palo Alto, Calif.: Science and Behavior Books, 1988).

[WEI93]   G.M. Weinberg, *Quality Software Management, Vol. 2: First-Order Measurement* (New York: Dorset House Publishing, 1993).

[WEI94]   ——, *Quality Software Management, Vol. 3: Congruent Action* (New York: Dorset House Publishing, 1994).

[WEI97]   ——, *Quality Software Management, Vol. 4: Anticipating Change* (New York: Dorset House Publishing, 1997).

FOUR

Language

We all speak different languages, even when we appear to be speaking the same words in the same language. These differences in what we *intend* to communicate with a specific word or phrase versus what the listener or reader understands us to have said result in miscommunications, mistakes, incorrect assumptions, and waste. Communication problems are common, it is true, but that does not mean we, as managers, should accept them as inevitable. We can and must learn to minimize their occurrence and negative effect. Managers, after all, are (sometimes) highly skilled translators, interpreting data from customers to producers to corporate heads.

I have always liked to communicate, especially in written form. By the time I was in college and working at the plant, I felt I was a fairly skilled writer and communicator. At the plant, though, people communicated in ways new to me, and I often struggled with what the words I heard were intended to mean. In retrospect, I see how little the men at the plant and I really "communicated," probably because we didn't have much in common to talk about—in terms of family background, education, and work and life experiences—so I guess I shouldn't have been surprised by these difficulties. What did surprise me was that when I began working as an engineer—as a "professional" in a field filled with other educated professionals—communication problems still existed.

Language difficulties occur less frequently for me now, in part because I have learned in recent years a three-step approach that eliminates most communication difficulties. Once I've taken the first step—the hardest for me—and admitted that I even have language difficulties, I take the next step, which focuses on developing my desire to do better—a step that takes humility and discipline. (For years I believed that *other* people needed to do better and considered myself to be a perfectly capable communicator.) The third step pushes me to use several different media to get my message across in every way possible.

One of the biggest problems I have in connection with language that is ambiguous or confusing comes from my tendency to assume that other people like what I like and know what I know. No matter how many times I find that just the opposite is true, I still seem to assume that people will quickly understand what I say and will agree with me. Such assumptions have caused me endless headaches and needless waste on the projects I have managed.

One way I find solutions to language differences is to ask the Data Question. Asking "What have I seen, read, or heard that leads me to believe that thus-and-such is true?" helps me to notice when I am making assumptions. The answers I get to the Data Question show me that I may be basing decisions on false assumptions.

In my workplace, we speak a common language (English), but our personal variations give each of us our own special slant to produce a not-so-common language. Despite being cognizant of the fact that the same words can express many different meanings, I find this both troublesome and beneficial. What is the reason for this? Well, when you and another person choose different ways of expressing what is basically the same idea, suddenly the impossible becomes possible as one person sparks another person's understanding of the situation and new opportunities arise.

THE HOSE-PIPE

In the beginning, working at the asphalt plant gave me a severe case of culture shock. A large part of this was due to the vocabulary people used. One early morning while I was standing next to the conveyor belts at the asphalt plant, Jackson, one of the front-end-loader operators, maneuvered his machine to a stop next to me and peered down from the cab with an expression on his face that let me know he wanted something. He yelled over the sound of the moving belts, falling rocks, and his idling motor, "Dwayne, hand me that pipe."

I looked around on the ground where he was pointing but I did not see anything remotely resembling a pipe. I gave him a puzzled look and the palms-up sign as I shouted back, "What?" He repeated his request. I again scanned the ground and then shot back another "What?"

Jackson pointed at a piece of garden hose that was coiled on the ground near where I was standing. When I picked up an end of the hose, Jackson's wide grin let me know I'd finally understood what he wanted.

Jackson and I were as different as two people could be, in physical appearance as well as in the vocabulary to which we proved partial. He was somewhere in his sixties at the time, was close to six-feet tall, and weighed more than three-hundred pounds. He'd grown up in segregated Mississippi during the Great Depression and, although he was a veteran of World War II, he'd never left Mississippi to fight for his country (people of color from the State of Mississippi were not sent off to fight alongside whites on the field of battle back then). With his few years of schooling, he could read, write, and do rudimentary math, and he'd long ago come to Louisiana to find work. As I came to know him, I saw him not in terms of physical appearance, education, or military credentials, but rather as a man with a kind spirit and an unquenchable desire to do good by others. Jackson was much more than the sum of his formal education.

As I stood beside the conveyor belts that day at the plant, holding the section of hose, I watched with alarm as Jackson shut off the front-end-loader's engine and struggled out of the cab. His height and weight made climbing down from the cab laborious, and I was embarrassed to watch him struggle.

Finally on the ground, Jackson caught his breath and puffed out, "That's it. I just need this pipe that's connected to the faucet." I gave him another confused look as he bent over, again a struggle, and turned on the faucet connected to the garden hose, aimed the nozzle at the front-end loader, and rinsed layers of dirt off the cab's windshield. Done with the task, he turned off the water, scaled his way back up into the cab, restarted the engine, and rumbled away.

I stood dumbfounded, asking myself, "Who ever heard of calling a hose a pipe?"

I have no idea what Jackson was thinking as he drove away, but it was probably something like, "What's wrong with young people nowadays? Don't they even understand English?"

The lesson I took from this episode of language culture-shock was the following:

We each speak our own language.

A Model of Communication

Jackson and I didn't communicate particularly well that morning during the hose-pipe exchange, and there would be many more, equally dumbfounding to me, cases of noncommunication during my days at the asphalt plant. I can explain most of those away as resulting from the vast cultural differences that existed between the men at the plant and myself.

I cannot, however, explain away the personal and professional miscommunications and misunderstandings that have occurred in my life in the ensuing years, when it has seemed as if another person and I were speaking different languages. Despite the fact that we face one another, speak words in English, and hear perfectly well, we give one another the same "What?" expression that I gave Jackson. Worse yet, sometimes I'm afraid to give the "What?" look. Instead, I pretend to understand what the other person is saying. Then I walk away, completely clueless, do what I think is best, and stand the chance of making a terrible mess.

Learning a more effective way to interact and communicate has helped me avoid misunderstanding what others tell me. It has also helped me avoid miscommunicating when I dispense information or instructions.

The model that works well for me is one devised by the late family therapist Virginia Satir (*see* [WEI86] *and* [WEI93] *for discussions of Satir and her research and writings).* The Satir Interaction Model has four basic steps: (1) Intake, (2) Meaning, (3) Significance, and (4) Response. *Intake* is information the listener takes into his or her mind. Note that this step is not called "input" as it is not what the speaker puts into the listener's mind.

Meaning is what the listener assigns to what he or she has taken in. This step has nothing to do with the person who is speaking; the listener is the only participant. (In my interaction with Jackson back at the plant, I took in the word "pipe" and believed it to mean "a metal tube with a diameter of a quarter-inch to several inches.")

The *Significance* step concerns the relevance that the listener assigns both to the speaker and to the meaning. In this step, *I* decide whether the specific interaction means anything (that is, whether it is relevant or significant) *to me.* Imagine an interaction in which a stranger walking by me on the sidewalk catches my eye and mumbles something to me. Neither the message nor the person has any significance for me. Now suppose I am at home, and my wife suddenly appears in the doorway to my office and mumbles something to me. I assign the same Meaning to my wife's mumbling as I did to the mumble of the stranger, but this interaction is Significant because it is with my wife and our relationship is important to me.

Notice how the Significance step relates to the particulars of the situation. The form of communication—a mumble—is the same in the two examples, but the time, place, and people are quite different. These differences radically change the Significance I assign to the interaction.

The final step in the Satir Interaction Model is *Response*, which factors in how the listener responds to the speaker. As listener, I can respond by doing nothing (as I did with the imaginary stranger on the imaginary sidewalk) or I can ask for a clarification of what was mumbled.

Applying the Satir Interaction Model retroactively to my interaction with Jackson, I see that the Meaning and Response steps started up again with my puzzled look as I held out my hands with my palms up. Jackson was the listener, and he assigned the Meaning that I intended ("Jackson, I don't understand what you want."). Cleaning his windshield was Significant to Jackson, so his Response was to climb down from his cab, grab the hose, turn on the water, and wash the dirt from the windshield.

FILTERS

For this discussion, I have simplified the Satir Interaction Model in order to make it easier to follow. There are, however, many components in addition to the four steps I've described. One—the concept of filters—is particularly important to any discussion of language.

I may be affected by "filters," things that sharpen or distort my ability to perform, at each step of the Model. Social rules are filters that affect communication. The rules tell me how to conduct myself in social interactions with other people. For example, "I must always agree with my grandparents (or anyone who reminds me of my grandparents)." "If I don't have anything complimentary to say, I must say nothing." "Children (or anyone who happens to feel like a child at the time) should only speak when spoken to." Other filters relate to the context of the interaction. Context includes the place (home, office, beach), the people involved, the day of the week, the time of day, and the season of the year.

The two types of filters that affect me most are *my past* and *my state of mind* during the interaction. My past keeps me from concentrating on the current interaction. Instead, I am driven by memories of other people and situations.

My past also acts as a filter when the person with whom I'm communicating reminds me of a third person who is not present. Remembering the third person keeps me from paying attention to the person with whom I now must communicate. The person-from-the-past filter hurt my business career in the mid-1980s when I met a character named Charlie. Something about Charlie reminded me of another person (unfortunately, someone I held in low regard). This memory caused me to dismiss Charlie as not worth the time of day. I heard what he said, thoughtlessly assigned it a Meaning, and gave it no Significance. My Response to Charlie was to avoid him and turn down the opportunity to discuss a business idea he wanted to propose.

Many months later, I learned that Charlie was an immensely successful businessman who managed large ventures in several different fields. Even if I hadn't chosen to join Charlie in any of his ventures, I believe I probably would have been well served for years to come by the knowledge he could have imparted in conversation. My person-from-the-past filter, however, kept me from listening and benefiting.

My state of mind is also a strong filter. Being happy, sad, scared, confident, or weary greatly influences how I interact with others. State of mind has affected me differently in different situations. My first job as a systems engineer gave me the opportunity to move my family clear across the country on short notice. We found a house we could afford, but it was in a rural location and it was going to require a lot of work. Our second child, Nathan, was a newborn and with Seth, then 22-months-old, kept my wife on the run 24/7, understandably leaving the lion's share of work on the house to me to try to tackle at the end of my workday.

To compound matters, I was in a type of job I had never done before, working with a group of people I did not know. I was tired and confused. So it would be an exaggeration to say that I was of sound mind when I met with two executives from a company that was supplier for a hundred or so major components of our system. I don't remember what they said in our meeting, but I do remember their somber looks. They were telling me something serious, to which I responded with a tired smile, "Well, okay. What else?"

I didn't have the Satir Interaction Model as a tool at that point in my career, but my Intake and Meaning facilitators were decidedly cloudy. My state of mind had filtered out all the important information. I am thankful that the two executives recognized my irrelevant response for what it was. I am also thankful that my very experienced technician was present during that meeting and was blessed with a clear and analytical mind, because what the executives were explaining to us was that their engineers had discovered a latent defect in their product.

The two executives told us that they needed to remove their components from our system, take them back to their facility, and repair them. They assured us that they would do this quickly and at no cost; they did not want to damage the good working relationship we had. This was a major announcement and it explained why two well-dressed, highly paid executives from a large company were paying a personal visit to this inexperienced, exhausted, confused systems engineer.

The situation ended well as the components' manufacturer did what the executives promised. It repaired the components quickly and quietly and the recall and fix did not disturb our delivery date, averting what surely could have been an all-out disaster for me as well as for my organization.

THAT'S SHOW BUSINESS

Back in the day, the team of Abbott and Costello performed a comedy routine I call "Who's on first?" Speaking in English, they might as well have been speaking Russian or Chinese for all I could make of the routine. To my view, the joke chased itself in vain with no conclusion.

I didn't appreciate the Abbott and Costello routine. It was insanely silly, intended to show how really stupid people had really stupid misunderstandings. Such silly misunderstandings would not occur in real life, I thought, certainly not in mine! After all, I listened well and I understood people. I spoke clearly, using well-chosen words so that others understood me. Misunderstandings were for other people.

Well, I was wrong. I had an attitude that demonstrated that I didn't understand the causes of miscommunication or misunderstanding. Everyone I have ever talked with about the subject has had more than a little experience with the morass of misunderstandings. Miscommunication doesn't just happen in connection with trivial things (such as someone calling something a garden hose while another someone calls the thing a pipe). It occurs in big business and, when it does, it costs millions of dollars.

One particular miscommunication cost me dearly in the mid-1990s when I was responsible for purchasing and maintaining the computer systems for a large processing laboratory. We used the Unix operating system on large computers (remember VAX minicomputers and Cray supercomputers?) and weren't ready to make the inevitable switch to PCs or Macs.

The miscommunication occurred when a mid-level manager came into my office and asked me a fairly straightforward question: "Do we need to buy one-hundred personal computers?" Although my Intake was the manager's nine simple words, the Meaning I assigned to the question took the following detour into what such a purchase would cost. What I concluded he was asking was, "Will we run into terrible problems doing all necessary computation if we don't buy one-hundred personal computers at a cost of three thousand dollars each?"

The $300,000 investment associated with such a purchase caused me to perk up immediately. I thought a moment, and then I responded with an assessment of what I believed our actual need was at that point in time: "Of course not. That would be a waste of money. We could use a half-dozen personal computers so we can connect to other types of systems—ones running on Windows operating systems, for example—but I don't see any call for one-hundred new machines."

The mid-level manager noted my answer and walked away satisfied. The lab got six PCs in due time, and we were able to put them to good use, coming to understand their ever-increasing popularity. I'd pretty much forgotten about the conversation until several months later when I received a call from a senior manager several levels above me in the organization. He was furious, spouting off at me over the phone line because he had just learned that, by my telling the mid-level manager that we only needed a half-dozen PCs, I had, in effect, turned down $282,000 in additional funding for our lab. He stated that we hadn't needed to buy all one-hundred PCs in order to receive the full $300,000 in funding. All I'd had to do was say Yes to the question asked several months earlier.

I felt that the senior manager was blaming the wrong person when he chewed me out, and so I tried to explain my point of view about the miscommunication in as calm a way as I could: The mid-level manager had not explained that we could receive the money without buying the PCs. I didn't succeed in convincing the senior manager, but I did learn a lesson.

Maybe it was the mid-level manager's fault or maybe it really was my fault, but the outcome was the same. The lab had lost $282,000 in funding because of a miscommunication. The majority of miscommunications happen this way. They happen among smart, well-meaning people, cost us dearly, and, in the worst of cases, we never even know they occurred.

A ROSE BY ANY OTHER NAME WOULD SMELL AS SWEET

With apologies to William Shakespeare, I continue to believe that although clear, unambiguous communication is difficult to do, it is doable. In fact, there are whole books on the subject to help people use language to better effect. One such book is Naomi Karten's *Communication Gaps and How to Close Them* (*see* [KAR02]), which treats the subject of communication gaps (and gaffs) in a lively and practical way.

A few practices have helped me communicate better in the years since the hose-pipe incident. As noted previously, the first step anyone must take to overcome the difficulties of communicating clearly is admitting to having the difficulties. I must admit that I am not a perfect communicator. Even after years of acknowledging this fact and practicing the techniques I have learned, I still catch myself believing that a conversation has been simple and that its meaning is clear enough for all parties to proceed with whatever action has been discussed. Only later do I smack my forehead and realize that I did not communicate what I intended to communicate.

The next step is to actually state an acknowledgment of communication difficulties. An appropriate declaration could be: "Understanding each other in this highly complex interaction may prove to be difficult, despite our best intentions. Please stop me at any time for clarification."

A case in point occurred some years ago when I entered into an outsourcing arrangement with a company thousands of miles away. All preliminary negotiations and all details about requirements for the work to be done were communicated by means of documents sent via fax machines. At the top of each page that I faxed to my contacts at the company, I wrote the message, "To write is to be misunderstood."

In retrospect, I can see that this message probably was a bit too cryptic, but I wanted the recipients of my fax to know that I would probably misunderstand some of their intended message and that they would probably misunderstand some of my intended message. I was on alert for areas of potential misunderstanding, and I wanted them to be the same. By writing this alert on each page of faxed material, I was hoping to avoid time- and resource-wasting assumptions. Once we cleared up what my message actually meant, the added note served us well.

One final tip I pass along to improve interaction: I encourage everyone to use as many forms of communication as possible.

When talking with another person face-to-face, I draw pictures or charts on a white board or on a sheet of paper. When I talk on the phone and cannot have a face-to-face discussion, I send a fax before the conversation so that the other person has a chance to read my message and preview any explanatory charts or pictures. If I send a fax or an e-mail, I follow up with a telephone call to discuss the content.

Thoughts on the Hose–Pipe

Trying to communicate with Jackson and the other men at the asphalt plant taught me many new uses for words, as well as new expressions and figures of speech. In spite of differences in age and education, we eventually managed to communicate pretty well. We did not cause or suffer any serious accidents while I was there, so I take that as proof that we communicated well enough to stay safe.

I remember the hose-pipe conversation to this day, but I also remember Jackson himself—as clearly as if we'd had the conversation only minutes ago. He was a cheerful, distinctive-looking man, with a few gold teeth in the front of his mouth that flashed and sparkled when he talked with anyone, primarily, I suppose, because he smiled and laughed much of the time, offering a happy countenance to the world. Jackson had learned how to communicate without the advantages of a Satir Interaction Model or an education based on reading and writing, and it was obvious even to a college kid like me that his kind, gentle, forgiving spirit and his love for people were greater assets than all the formal learning in the books.

Thinking back on how Jackson affected people who came into contact with him, I can see that those attributes—kindness, gentleness, forgiveness, love—have everything to do with communicating. We each may speak our own language, but attributes such as the ones that Jackson possessed somehow allow us to understand each other's language better.

SIGNING WITH AN X

One of the jobs I especially liked at the Louisiana Paving Company was known as "writing tickets." I'd sit by a window in the company's control room and wait for dump-truck drivers to pull their asphalt-loaded dump trucks onto a scale outside my window so that their load could be weighed and purchased.

A mechanical calculator in the control room read the weight registered on the scale, and then subtracted the on-file "empty weight" for the particular truck from the registered weight of the now-fully-loaded truck. It then printed out a paper tape showing the difference between the two numbers—the weight of the asphalt in the load—along with the date and time.

Reading the tape, I would write the information on a multi-copy receipt in a "ticket book," pull an original and a copy from the book, and staple them to the calculator tape. I then would attach the stapled papers to a string and slide the papers-and-string contraption down a chute to the waiting driver. The driver usually would check the data for accuracy, initial both copies of the ticket, attach one copy to the string, and keep the other copy for his records. I then pulled the string back up the chute and put the signed receipt in a box for the accountant to record and invoice the next day. I liked this job because it was systematic and rewardingly methodical—and because it seemed to work flawlessly.

One day when I was writing tickets, a small dump truck from the Parish pulled in with a load of asphalt to be weighed. As always, the calculator printed the paper tape, I wrote the information into the ticket book, and then I slid the stapled batch of papers down the chute to the waiting driver. I turned away to check on the box of receipts left over from the previous day and quickly became absorbed in the task. I was startled a few moments later when the driver walked slowly up to the control room with a pencil and the papers in hand. He held the papers out to me and asked where he should sign. I didn't understand why he was asking, but I pointed to the line that had the word "Signature" and an "X" next to it.

The driver held the pencil awkwardly, marking an X on the signature line of both copies of the receipt. In somewhat a state of disbelief, I slowly pulled the papers apart, handed him his receipt, and watched him walk down the stairs and back to his truck.

This was 1979. This man had a driver's license—in fact, a special license to operate heavy equipment—but it appeared that he couldn't read or write or even sign his name. As a kid, I had seen

Westerns on TV where some of the cowboys of the 1800s "made their mark"—an X—on papers, but I really didn't believe that to be correct historically because I imagined that, even in the 1800s, most Americans could sign their name. I was wrong about the Westerns and was shocked to see further evidence in 1979.

I learned from this driver who signed his name with an X:

Things we think can no longer exist still do.

SOME THINGS THAT CANNOT STILL EXIST DO STILL EXIST

Situations I once naïvely thought no longer existed in fact still exist. On that day at the plant, the driver marked an X and opened my eyes to the recognition that certain conditions and behaviors that I assumed had gone the way of the dodo bird are very much alive.

When I assume that something no longer can occur, I cause problems in two respects. First, I do my customers an injustice because I limit myself to seeing only what I assume is in keeping with their abilities and needs. I have a preconceived notion about the way things are, rather than opening my eyes to what might be. In so doing, I fail to serve my customers.

Second, by assuming things that can or cannot be, I shut down my coworkers, stifling their creativity and limiting their productivity as well as my own. Such behavior prevents us from reaching together for the stars in order to create the highest quality products.

We see less evidence in the modern world that areas of breathtaking, natural beauty still exist—glaciers are melting, rain forests are shrinking, for example—but breathtakingly beautiful places still can be viewed in every country in the world. Such places do still exist.

Cultures in which citizens show respect for their elders and for authority still exist in every society. Products such as pencils and paper are still the implements of choice for some. These are persistent, sustaining elements that time does not erase. Even though we don't think their existence possible in modern culture, these elements are not extinct.

My task as a manager is to keep in mind that all manner of things still exist. This way of thinking enables me to work *with people* to create systems and services *for people.*

ASSUMING AND FORGETTING

I am a person who tends to assume many things. For example, I assume that all guns are loaded, that the food in restaurants is safe to eat, that the lights will come on in my house when I flip the switch, and that my mini-van will start when I turn the key. There is little harm in these assumptions.

Most of my assumptions stem from my having some bit of data. I face a problem, I work out the answer, and I go with it. Since I "know" the answer, there is no need to check on my conclusions. I don't need to ask for clarification, I don't need to think again, and I certainly don't need to ask a colleague to review my solution before I act on it.

Many assumptions I have made over the years have brought me trouble. Assuming that people will listen to me and do what I recommend (because I am smart and educated and everyone can see that my advice is correct!) has caused me no end of grief.

Author and consultant Jerry Weinberg writes about the central dogma of academic psychology, which asserts that there is one correct solution to every problem and the psychologist knows it (*see* [WEI98]). I didn't know about the central dogma of academic psychology until I read Weinberg, but I certainly let my own home-grown version of it rule my actions. Once I saw a solution to a problematic situation, I was done. I assumed that my solution was the one and only. Worse yet, I assumed that everyone else would see my solution as the only reasonable approach.

The opposite of the central dogma is the belief that there is always another answer to a question, another resolution to a problem. (Before concluding a discussion or settling on a solution, I rein in a bit, reminding myself, "Maybe I haven't found enough possible solutions yet; maybe I should think a while longer.")

At this point in my career—and in my personal life as well—I now try to think of at least three solutions to each situation. Next, I try to think of reasons why doing the opposite of my three possible solutions could also be reasonable ways to solve the problem. Then, I discuss my six possible approaches with other people. If they don't support the validity of all six solutions (or a subset of the six), I try to think of three reasons why they might be right.

Finding six possible solutions to every problem and then three reasons why any or all of the solutions I've proposed are not validated by my colleagues and staff (or my management, or my family, or my friends) may seem like an awful lot of work to go to just to avoid making the wrong decision or an unsupportable assumption. That's true, but searching for multiple answers to each question and multiple solutions to each problem has helped me both grow and do a better job in every arena of my life.

But *forgetting* accompanies assuming. At times, I forget that there was a day when I didn't know some of the things that I know now, and so I assume that everyone knows what I know. The obvious truth is that there was a time when I, for example, didn't know how to sign my name, didn't know my right from my left, couldn't punch a sequence of buttons to open a combination lock, didn't know my colors. It seems silly to need to remind myself of this, but there are days when I forget that I had to learn these things.

In forgetting, my assumption that other people know what I know takes front stage and steers me astray. To counter the bad habit of assumption, I remind myself that other people need the opportunity to learn, just as I had the opportunity. As a result, I make far fewer assumptions about people today, although my transition has been slow and, sometimes, painful.

FEARING, FORGETTING, AND ASSUMING

I'd also forgotten what it was like to feel fear and uncertainty as a child. Until someone reminded me recently, I had forgotten the fear that comes when kids pick teams to play ball, for example. My fears were manifold: Would I be picked last for the team? Would I be picked at all? Would I cry if ridiculed by the other kids for a dropped ball or a missed catch?

I had also forgotten the fear and uncertainty that comes when asking a girl out for a date. Again, my fears and anxieties were many: Will she go out with me? Will she laugh and tell her friends that I have been silly enough to ask her? What will my friends think of me for liking this particular girl? Where will we go and what will I talk about if she accepts my invitation?

Now, as an adult responsible for managing a staff and for developing and delivering systems and services to customers, I must remind myself again and again that the workplace itself stirs up fear and anxiety in many people. If I do not take their fears, uncertainties, and other feelings into consideration, I will not serve them well.

I learned another lesson about fear and anxiety in the workplace in the early 1990s when my organization planned to switch all employees from using text-only word processors to graphical word processors. Back then, text-only word processors showed green text against a black screen and the only way to move the cursor was by touching the arrow keys.

The planned change to Windows and a mouse was a big one, but I had forgotten just how big because I had made the move five years earlier. Having typed on keyboards for fifteen years prior to that move, I found that taking my hands off the keyboard to operate a mouse in order to direct the cursor required heavy-duty concentration and reprogramming of my seemingly hard-wired instincts.

But I had forgotten all that when I was asked to help my organization to make the switch. I simply assumed that everyone would welcome the opportunity to push away the old text-based processors and move forward. I stopped feeling this way when I sat with a secretary to train her to use the new word processor. She had been typing on keyboards for close to thirty years and she froze in terror—seeming almost paralyzed—whenever she needed to take her hands off the keyboard to move the mouse.

When verbal instruction and patient encouragement failed to free her from her fear, I literally put my hand on top of hers to move her hand and the mouse that controlled the cursor appearing on the screen. Our first lesson lasted three hours, at the end of which, both she and I were perspiring, exhausted from the effort expended. She and everyone else in the organization eventually made the change to Windows and a mouse, but I never again forgot the lesson of how hard it can be to learn something new when fear and anxiety interfere.

FINDING THE DINOSAURS

Dinosaurs are extinct—everyone knows that. My trouble is, I cannot prove that statement to be true. It *is* true that no one during the past several hundreds of years has brought a living creature in front of the public and proved it to be a member of the group Dinosauria. But it is possible that dinosaurs exist in some remote part of the planet. I admit that the probability is low, but, given that I cannot prove that there are no dinosaurs simply because no one alive today has seen one, the probability is greater than zero.

I can claim that one thing or another doesn't exist, but if my claim is based solely on the fact that I've not seen whatever it is, I might as well keep quiet and focus on discovering what things that I thought no longer existed still do exist. When I know that, I can do a better job of building and managing systems and services with and for people.

My most successful discoveries come from asking questions. When I think I "know" something, I check my knowledge by asking myself the Data Question: "What have I seen, read, or heard that leads me to believe that thus-and-such is true?" I answer this question best when I allow enough time for thought.

Sometimes, this means several minutes; sometimes, several weeks. Sometimes, I become lazy and settle for an incorrect answer to the Data Question that comes with little effort, an answer based on things I hear during conversations at work and in commentaries on the radio. These tidbits stay in my mind and often become "facts" that I know. I promise myself that I will do some research and learn the whole truth instead of just settling for what I hear. Too often, however, I skip the research step and jump to the "I know" state of mind.

Sometimes, I ask the Data Question and then proceed to the research phase. Research often gives me answers I don't want to accept. There are people who don't think like me, don't act like me, don't feel like me, and don't like the things I like, so I need to be very careful not to dismiss the valuable answers my research shows, especially if I am biased against their source.

Over time, I've learned that I work best with and for people when I know them. Sometimes, I stand back and watch people, as I've discussed previously. Through observation, I can discover all sorts of things, but sometimes I presume things about people by observing their external appearance, which isn't a reliable indicator of the person's values, beliefs, and true character. Observation is valuable, but incomplete.

Asking direct questions of people *about themselves* (asking, for example, what are their likes and dislikes, what is their community like, what is their preferred way to spend a day off) is the best method I know for gathering answers to the Data Question. My questions run from the deeply personal, such as, "What do you believe?" "What is your preferred lifestyle?" "What are you like?" and "How would you describe yourself?" to less-personal, work- and surroundings-related questions, such as, "What do you do?" "What places do you like to go to for entertainment?" "For meals out?" "What is your community like?" "What kinds of hobbies do you enjoy?" The last question I ask is open-ended: "Is there anything else you would like to tell me about yourself?" Knowing these details about the person *as an individual* helps me to analyze the answers the person will tell me.

There is plenty of danger in asking other people personal questions, and some danger in asking broad questions that are related to the person's profession. Some people won't answer candidly—for reasons I may never know. I find that the best approach for me is to be open and honest. I try to set the tone by saying something like, "I want to do well in this situation. I don't know you yet, and I don't do well when I don't have context. It would help me to work with you if you would share information with me. I have a bunch of questions that I hope you will answer either now or at some time when you feel comfortable doing so. If I ask a question that you don't want to answer, please just say so." When I've finished asking my questions, I invite the person to ask the same or other questions of me, so that we are on even footing.

RIDING THE DINOSAURS

It interests me greatly to *know* that things I thought no longer exist still do. I think of these things as "exceptions" because, unlike most things that I think no longer exist, these exceptions do. *Knowing*, however, is only the first step. The next challenge is using the answers and solutions I gather to correct my erroneous "knowledge." I must put aside my fear and bias, integrate the solutions and answers into what I "know," and, if necessary, throw away my assumptions.

People have the ability to handle exceptions because they can assess the "rule," as well as the exception to it, and make a decision based on any number of tangible and intangible factors. Systems—whether technical, physical, or social—have little success dealing with exceptions because systems generally are inflexible and unwieldy—and they cannot come easily to a consensus regarding the action to take. Most impasses and deadlocks I encounter end when some person says, "This is an exceptional case. I've thought about it and this is what I've decided we can do."

Take, for example, the somewhat unusual situation of one colleague who falls asleep in meetings. In most gatherings, the system of meetings exists on the "rule" that everyone must sit quietly around a conference table and listen, until called upon to speak. This man had a physical condition such that when he sat still for longer than ten minutes, his blood didn't circulate properly and he fell asleep. Because he worked a desk job, he could move as often as necessary and still do his job, but in meetings, he sat as still as he could to show respect for the speaker and to fit in with the norm. Sitting still for the duration of our meetings caused him to fall asleep.

We had several choices about how to work with him. One possibility was to amend the rule about sitting quietly with an exception: ". . . except when a person has a physical condition and falls asleep when sitting still for more than ten minutes."

That would work. The problem was that every time we met another exception, we would have to amend the rule with another long set of careful words. Writing exceptions to rules takes a lot of time and energy.

As a manager, I try to combine the best attributes of man-made systems and people. A system can work for most cases, but people are needed to handle and understand the exceptions. We can have our rule for meeting conduct, but if someone wants to attend and cannot abide by our rule, we will work with the needs of the exceptional person.

Thinking about extinction, rules, and exceptions has had a profound effect on me. I see a flashing red light whenever I hear someone speak in absolute terms, such as, "We don't have to consider that any more. No one does that any more. Everyone knows that now." These statements are variations of "That thing doesn't exist any more." The first thing I think when hearing an absolute is that the statement is probably wrong, and I ask myself, "What would it mean if that absolute were false?"

For example, what would it mean if dinosaurs still roamed the Earth? Could we domesticate the brontosaurus and use him as a source of protein to feed starving people (thereby hastening true extinction)? Could we ride the pterodactyl like a horse and provide transportation to people without burning fossil fuels?

Back to the more probable, what would it mean if there were many people who look like they can sign their name, but who are really just making a fancy X? How would this affect our educational system? What would it mean if most people who sit quietly in meetings were only pretending to pay attention while they were really thinking of great ideas that they would implement if they were CEO? How would this affect our company practices?

As a manager, it's my job to think of ideas that help my colleagues and staff work together to produce better systems. I've found that reversing absolutes helps me generate ideas. Looking for the next person who signs his name with an X has led me to good ideas throughout the years.

Thoughts on Signing a Name

I met many dump-truck drivers in my years at the asphalt plant, but I don't remember particulars about most of them. The man who signed his name with an X is one of the few I do remember well. He had a frightened look on his face as he handed me the papers and asked me where to sign. As I pointed to the line on each copy of the receipt, I struggled to guess why he had to ask such a question. Being functionally illiterate was not one of the possibilities I had considered.

CONCLUSIONS

People possess qualities and are endowed with characteristics and traits that I cannot imagine, let alone assume I understand. There is something that is an exception to the rule about every person. Discovering what is exceptional helps me develop my ability to provide systems and services for others. Sometimes, it also helps me discover exceptional things about myself. Among the lessons I learned from Driver X are

We each speak our own language.

Things we think can no longer exist still do.

REFERENCES

[KAR02] N. Karten, *Communication Gaps and How to Close Them* (New York: Dorset House Publishing, 2002).

[WEI86] G.M. Weinberg, *Becoming a Technical Leader: An Organic Problem-Solving Approach* (New York: Dorset House Publishing, 1986).

[WEI93] ——, *Quality Software Management, Vol. 2: First-Order Measurement* (New York: Dorset House Publishing, 1993).

[WEI98] ——, *The Psychology of Computer Programming: Silver Anniversary Edition* (New York: Dorset House Publishing, 1998).

FIVE

Culture

Culture describes patterns of human activity. It shapes who we are, what we do, and how we do it. Although it is sometimes difficult to see what our own culture is like when we are immersed in it, doing so can help us realize that the ways we live and do things are only some of many ways of living and doing. Often, the way we do things becomes the way we *should* do them. If, however, we take notice of our own culture and observe how it differs from others, we can open our minds to new ways of living and doing—and that can change our management practices for the better.

When I saw things at the asphalt plant that were different from the way I knew, I felt as if I were in a foreign land, trying to learn about bizarre practices happening around me. The unusual ways of doing things weren't all bad, so I learned to catch my breath and go on with the day. In the early months, I discovered something new almost every day. As I became acclimated, I saw that the new ways worked just as well as the ones I knew.

During those days at the plant and my subsequent stints working in half-a-dozen different countries on four continents, I was reminded time and time again that the norm for one culture can seem bizarre to another, and that being in a strange environment helps most everyone to better see their own.

Sandwich Surprises

I've stated that a part of culture is the way we do things, but one of my first experiences at the plant was learning that differences in culture can even run to sandwiches. During my second or third week at the plant, I sat down to eat lunch with Jackson just as he pulled a fist-sized white mound out of a large paper bag. I thought it was a sandwich, but it was round instead of flat. I already knew that Jackson loved to eat and that he wasn't a finicky eater, but I couldn't imagine what this thing was that he had brought for lunch.

As Jackson wrapped his hands around the object and began to eat, I saw that it was two slices of white bread squashed around a piece of fried chicken. This wasn't your everyday, fried, boneless chicken breast, however; it was a fried chicken *back*, with bones and all. Jackson crunched the sandwich and swallowed everything while I tried not to show that I was dumbfounded.

In the ensuing days, I saw Jackson eat other "sandwiches." He would squeeze white bread over whatever he brought with him—and he had himself a sandwich. I saw him eat a pork-chop sandwich, a fish sandwich, and some kind of featherless, small-bird sandwich—and every one of these sandwiches included bones, skin, and whatever came with the center section. I had seen what I considered to be odd combinations consumed as sandwiches before—scrambled-egg, tomato, American cheese, and mayonnaise on white bread, for example—but bone-and-skin-filled sandwiches were new to me.

In hindsight, Jackson was about thirty years ahead of his time. Nowadays, people slap bread around things that don't resemble my idea of a sandwich. Restaurants call these things "wraps," and they offer salad wraps, chicken-and-rice wraps, steak-and-bean wraps—you name it. For all I know, there may even be fruit wraps and cereal wraps. I suppose Jackson invented the wrap, but I'm pretty sure he never received credit for it.

Whether he got inventor's credit or not, Jackson caused me to reconsider my concept of a sandwich. I now saw that I could put anything edible between two pieces of bread and call it a sandwich. That was using the basic concept of the sandwich and extending it. I thought of many things that would be okay to eat that way, but I'll probably stick with peanut butter and jelly. I'm just not really a sandwich man.

Jackson probably wasn't really a sandwich man either, but he lived in a culture that was different from mine. His home culture knew about the "anything" sandwich, while mine only knew of a few limited sandwiches. This taught me a lesson about culture and common items:

A different culture can reveal a new set of possibilities.

The experience with Jackson and his sandwiches spurred me to observe closely while amid different cultures. When I subsequently worked and lived in Hong Kong, Nigeria, and Pakistan, I hoped to see and learn from other common objects used in ways I wouldn't have imagined.

HONG KONG

The culture of the Chinese people is very different from that of, say, the American South. For example, the Chinese language has different words for different relationships. Instead of saying, "This person is my third son," Chinese people have a word meaning "third son." They also have distinct words to differentiate "my brother's son" from "my sister's son."

I spent many months in Hong Kong, and one lesson I took from the Chinese language is, when something is important, give it its own name. When a concept has its own name, people work with it better than when it is just a combination of ideas. Where I work, people give names to projects. That helps us differentiate between them and know precisely which project someone is discussing. A name transforms a project from "that thing Chuck is working on" to the Engineering Management Team (EMT). We can discuss the EMT because it has a name that represents something specific to us.

Chinese culture differs from my own in that it pays great attention to the daily meal. For centuries, the vast majority of Chinese people have lived in poverty. Mealtime became the most important part of daily life because without a daily meal, a person could die. The importance of the meal is expressed in a common Chinese greeting. Instead of saying, "Hello, how are you?" some Chinese people say, "Have you eaten?" If the other person answers Yes, he must be doing well because he has consumed a meal that day.

The Chinese respect their food as well. Instead of inventing new dishes, the Chinese have a small number of established dishes. They prepare their meals according to recipes that are several thousand years old. Deviating from this would show disrespect for their ancestors and to the meal. Once the meal is prepared, the Chinese stop what they are doing and enjoy the experience to its fullest.

Before my exposure to Chinese culture, I often rushed through meals, especially during the workday. I practiced the American tradition of grabbing a burger, shoving it into my mouth, and keeping on doing whatever else there was to do. I usually ate this way at work, and I was repulsed by the thought of a long, slow meal breaking up the day. Working with my Chinese counterparts in Hong Kong showed me that my mealtime practice was probably costly to my employer and threatened doom on projects.

Observing Chinese culture caused me to change the way I think about mealtime. Now, I see that meals can serve as a special time in the day for interacting in a relaxed way with people, especially in the workplace. I gain much by enjoying a leisurely lunch with coworkers and other business associates. In fact, whenever I work on outsourcing projects, I try to visit my contractors once a month, and I make a point of taking time to have lunch with them. The meals aren't special because of the great ham-and-cheese sandwiches; they are special because they make it possible for me to get to know the contractors *as individuals,* who have families and outside interests. An added benefit (from my point of view, at least) is that the contractors learn similar details about me. These projects always seem to progress better after we've enjoyed a few meals together.

NIGERIA

I lived in Lagos for two years and quickly observed firsthand how vastly different the West African culture is from that of my homeland. For example, West Africans speak about inanimate objects as if they are living creatures. Hotel maids do not "make up the bed." Instead, they "lay down the bed," as if the sheets and covers were alive. West Africans call a flat tire "a car foot out of breath," giving cars human parts and capabilities.

I initially thought that this practice was primitive and that it had no counterpart in Western culture, but a closer analysis of the kinds of expressions people use in my profession changed my mind. Phrases like "projects take on a life of their own" and "this system is my baby" assign life to inanimate things just as the West African expressions do.

Nigerians put a different value on the merit of completing work projects versus building and maintaining strong personal relationships than most Westerners would assign. The Nigerians taught me that projects are just "things we do," but people are real, with relationships being much more important than the things we do. The message I heard loud and clear during my years in Nigeria was that, yes, Westerners can bring good to a Nigerian community by helping complete projects such as building roads, bridges, and airports, but they don't have to neglect people while doing so.

Nigerian guards at our housing compound in Lagos astonished me with their emphasis on putting people first. By my family's second day in residence, every one of the guards knew and could address me by my name. Within another couple of days, they knew the names of my wife and three sons, the times of day that we preferred to come and go, our individual preferences regarding public and private transportation, and many other things about us that made life easier and more pleasant for us. I thought that if Nigerians were able to learn details about my family and me so quickly, they must also be capable of learning how to complete work projects like building roads.

A Nigerian who had lived several years in America helped me understand this puzzle. He told me that he had seen this difference from the opposite side while living in America. He had noticed that Americans were able to conceive of and complete complex projects, but he'd met very few who could remember the names of neighbors who had lived next door to them for however many years. He had been shocked to observe that few of the Americans he met in the States knew more than the first name of their long-time auto mechanic, butcher, or dry cleaner. To a Nigerian, that was exceedingly odd. The answer, he concluded, was that Nigerians value relationships above all else, but Americans and other Westerners value projects above all else.

I didn't like the implications of his answer. I had to admit that I was one of those Westerners who put projects and accomplishments before people. I would come to be amazed a few months later when I witnessed Nigerian workers and project leaders letting a project slip a few days in order to ensure a good relationship with a coworker. They even halted the project—stopped it completely!—to help one coworker tend to a sick relative. I don't know if I ever could do that, and I've certainly never worked for a project manager who would do that either, but there is a lot to be learned from a culture that does.

PAKISTAN

In Pakistan, my experience with cultural differences, strangely enough, had to do with a job I had first learned at the asphalt plant—mixing concrete. Because I knew I was only going to be in Pakistan for a couple of months, I spent a good bit of my spare time exploring small towns and villages, hoping to get some insight into the country and its people. One day, when I was walking through some of the shops in a small village, I came upon a boy mixing concrete directly on the ground outside one of the shops.

I was fascinated by how this teenager was able to work without a wheel barrel or any type of flat container. He started by mounding powder and rocks into a pile on a smooth section of hard-packed dirt, and then he made a hole in the center of his pile and poured a small amount of water into it. This gave him enough moisture to mix the powder, rocks, and water into a concrete-like substance, but I could easily see that the concoction was too dry to use. Next, he made another hole in the center, poured in a little more water, and mixed things again. He repeated the process until he had a mass of shimmering concrete at just the right consistency, which he then used to patch a section of floor inside the shop where he worked.

I remained outside, amazed at having seen him succeed in mixing concrete, despite the approach and tools he had used. I had mixed concrete myself on several occasions at the asphalt plant. There, I had learned that one essential tool for mixing a batch of concrete is a wheel barrel or other similar, wide, flat container with sides, in which to combine the powder, rocks, and water. I had also learned that mixing the powder and rocks with water should be done in one step, because once the water hits the powder, it starts a reaction. My experience told me that adding small portions of water in several steps, the way the Pakistani teenager had done, should not have worked.

I had also doubted that the boy would be able to keep the mixed concrete from flowing away and hardening as it spread. Once mixed, concrete has the consistency of a very thick milk-shake, and I anticipated that, without a container with sides, the mixture would soon disperse. The teenager, however, didn't understand that his approach and tools were "problems." He mixed his concrete without a wheel barrel, and used the concrete he'd made to do the job.

The Pakistani boy had completed a first-rate project without what I considered to be an essential tool. Right at that moment, I realized that my notion of *essential* needed to change. Thinking about the episode, I wondered what other things that I consider to be essential are really not essential.

Asking myself this question on an almost daily basis since that day in 1981, I have learned that, among other things, thick documents are not essential to project success, meeting rooms are not essential to productive meetings, many words are not essential to effective communication, and well-structured organizations are not essential to accomplish work. I have also learned that when someone says, "We need to have X to do Y," I should ask whether X is really essential. After all, I saw a mere teenager mix concrete without a wheel barrel.

SEEING THE WORLD ON A DOLLAR A DAY

I have benefited enormously from living and working in foreign countries. I do understand, however, that not everyone has either the opportunity or the desire to live and work in the places I've been. For those people, the benefit of experiencing a different culture just as readily can be gleaned without their traveling any physical distance at all. In fact, pretty much anybody can enjoy short-distance travel to foreign cultures and learn a great deal.

Take my travel some years ago from Los Angeles into neighboring Orange County, for example. I used to think that cultural differences between people from different areas would increase in direct proportion to the miles between them, but crossing the county line between Los Angeles and Orange instantaneously took me into a radically different culture. A few decades ago, when I first crossed from L.A. to Orange, the difference was easy to see: Orange County had orange groves, agriculture, and salt-of-the-earth farmers; Los Angeles had concrete, industry, and high-flying celebrities. The difference is not quite so easy to see now—the physical surroundings are pretty close to being the same in both places: concrete, freeways, and strip malls.

The difference that does still exist between Orange County and Los Angeles can be seen in the attitude of the people in each area. Los Angeles is a big city with a big-city attitude (stereotypically, neighbors rarely know each other, people commute long distances that make quality family-time difficult to enjoy, and many inhabitants and tourists appear to value high-priced status symbols over small-town pleasures). Much of Orange County has a we're-not-L.A. attitude, which its people show by thinking and doing according to small-town, agricultural values. Orange County seems to have retained a culture vastly different from the county next door because *it chooses to do so.*

TRAVELING LESS THAN A MILE

The cultural disparity between Los Angeles and Orange County is evident despite a distance of only a few miles between them. In my Virginia neighborhood, I can step into a different culture after traveling even fewer miles. I experience this culture change while coaching my teenage sons, other teenagers from the neighborhood, and some kids from economically disadvantaged neighborhoods in basketball. Basketball is an up-close sport, and I can see the expressions on the kids' faces and hear what they mumble under their breath even when I'm coaching from the sidelines. Teenagers today have a different language, attitude, manner, and code of conduct than what I knew growing up. While I do have the title "Coach," I am merely a visitor in their teenage culture.

One lesson I learned while visiting their world during basketball-coaching sessions pertains to management ideas and exceptional people. It is the norm in our recreational league that one of two kids on a team have abilities and skills far beyond those of everyone else on their team. In such cases, the accepted theories of coaching do not hold. The exceptional players dominate, regardless of the game plans that I devise. Since noticing this in kids' basketball, I have also noticed it in the professional world. When one person on a project has exceptional ability, things that accepted practice would tell me should not work often do work.

This observation has taught me to be aware of several things. First, I have learned to be skeptical when someone lauds a new technique and holds up successful projects as proof of the effectiveness of the amazing new technique. Often the success is due to the personal ability of one individual instead of to application of the miraculous new technique.

Second, some managers succeed in spite of poor management techniques. Their success does not prove that their practices are acceptable. Instead, their success probably means that a few exceptional people were working on their project.

Third, when I begin a new project, I must think carefully about the people on the project before choosing how to manage it. If an exceptional person is onboard, I generally choose to back away and inject very little of my own managerial oversight. I, like most managers, must avoid becoming too enamored with my own ability as manager. If the few exceptional people leave the project, so may the magic.

TRAVELING TO THE LAND OF TINTED HAIR AND SHINY STUDS

Being part of a different culture in a different environment generally helps me to perform certain kinds of tasks better. An example dear to me while drafting this book was my local Starbucks. On average, I worked on drafts of this book five to ten hours a week, many of them spent in Starbucks coffee shops. I am not really a Starbucks fanatic, and I don't usually treat myself to fancy coffee concoctions whose names I cannot pronounce. But, for me anyway, writing sometimes calls for a different setting, and so I took myself to town.

At some of the Starbucks I frequent, many of the customers—as well as the youngsters behind the counter—sport vibrantly colored streaks in spiked hair; tattoos up and down what can be seen of their bodies (a lot); and shiny studs piercing their noses, ears, and heaven-only-knows what other places. My norm is coffee in a Styrofoam cup dispensed from a gas-station vending machine. Stepping into Starbucks, I step into a foreign culture.

Amazingly, I found that I could write my book drafts more easily in those Starbucks. I'm an engineer and writing is not a task I normally perform. I had struggled writing even a fleshed-out outline for certain sections of this book, but at Starbucks, I found the words.

I noticed something else at Starbucks: As the weeks passed and my drafts evolved into something I could submit to my publisher, I was still visiting Starbucks. Overhearing more conversations between people standing in line for coffee or serving from behind counters, I realized that, apart from the contemporary slang they used, their conversation topics were much like those I explored with kids in the 1970s at the Loranger Drive-In, back in Tangipahoa Parish.

The Starbucks kids had the same fears and dreams as the sons and daughters of dairy farmers I used to know. Starbucks began to be familiar to me, comfortable even—a home of a sort. I suspect that if I had visited too frequently, I would have lost the tension that comes in a foreign culture—and with it, the ability to write those difficult passages. It is possible for a foreign culture to lose its special qualities by becoming too familiar, too mundane. Therefore, if a place has great benefits to me because it is foreign in some fashion, I now know that I shouldn't visit it too often.

TRAVELING IN TIME

One way I found to explore a foreign culture without traveling any distance is to work different hours. For a while, I tried shifting my day by three hours (I came in three hours later and stayed three additional hours at night). I traveled the same roads, went in and left by the same door, and worked the same job, but the three-hour shift pushed me into a different culture. The traffic was different, the parking lot was different, and the people with whom I walked through the door were different. I saw the same things, but different people were using them in different ways.

Another simple way I initiate a culture shift is to dress differently for work or recreation. On rare occasions, I wear a black suit, white shirt, and black tie to my office. People look at me and speak to me differently. I find myself acting differently and seeing things from a different perspective.

I now know many ways to step into a different culture. These adventures include renting a different make and model of car, paying for everything with cash instead of by credit card or check, and using a wooden pencil exclusively instead of a pen or mechanical pencil. These and other small changes are simple tricks to illuminate common objects with a different light, and they generally help me to expand my ideas about the world and what happens in it.

Thoughts on Sandwiches

I'll never forget coming to the realization that Jackson was eating a fried chicken-back sandwich. It's odd how something that happened so long ago can stay in my memory, but that one lunch break has helped me to observe and learn new things almost every day since. It is still easy for me to get stuck in the validity of my own ideas about things, but remembering chicken-back sandwiches jolts my normal routine and allows me to expand my notion of how things are and how things just may be.

As a manager, I sometimes have the opportunity to investigate other cultures and put their ideas and practices to work for me, no matter where they come from. Even in the midst of a large, hectic project, I sometimes allow myself to step into other environments—for a break, for inspiration, for insight.

In retrospect, I see that my days at the asphalt plant were an immersion in a foreign culture. Simple, everyday experiences revealed many new possibilities to me—the education I got was priceless—although I didn't know that at the time.

Two Sets of Rules

Louisiana Paving Company was a private-sector company that contracted much of its work with the State of Louisiana. The company owned its trucks and equipment and competed for contracts with the State to pave and overlay roads. Under these contracts,

LPC had to abide by State regulations, including the regulation that dump trucks transporting loads of asphalt had to keep the load covered with a tarpaulin during inclement weather. This practice, which helped preserve the consistency of the asphalt, was important because when rain fell on the asphalt, it created a thin, hard crust on the top. That crust did not pack as well on the road, and this caused the road to deteriorate more quickly. The rules imposed by the State forced Louisiana Paving to build a culture of quality.

LPC also sold asphalt to road crews manned by employees of the State. State crews would buy asphalt from LPC and use it to patch potholes and to do other small jobs. The State crews didn't cover their loads of asphalt when it rained; in fact, they didn't even carry tarps on their trucks.

There were other differences between what LPC was required to do and what the State crews got away with. When our crews patched holes in a road, we first poured tack—pure liquid asphalt—into the hole. The tack acted as a glue to help hold the asphalt mixture in the hole. If someone filled a hole with asphalt without first adding tack, the pothole reappeared quickly. State crews never put tack into the potholes they filled. They just dumped the asphalt mixture into the hole and tapped it down with a shovel. Their patch jobs didn't last long at all.

The biggest difference, however, was with the inspectors. When our crews worked on roads, an inspector—an employee of the State—would stand at the job site and inspect the work. Once a day, the inspector would take a core sample from the road we were paving. He first would cut a circular hole that went down six-to-eight inches and then he would remove the road sample to send it back to the asphalt plant for testing. There, another State employee would separate the materials chemically to determine whether we were using the proper mixture of materials in our asphalt. State crews never had an inspector watch them for quality of work, and I never saw anyone test core samples from State jobs.

I eventually came to understand what seemed to be going on. The State had two sets of rules—one for commercial enterprises and another for its own workers. I later found the same disparity when I became an employee of the United States government. Government contractors were bound by many rigorous rules, regulations, and standards of work, but most government workers were not required to work according to those same rules, regulations, and standards. In those situations, government employees seemed to believe they were only being given *advice*—not requirements—on how the work should be performed. They behaved as do many individuals who receive advice, choosing to follow it or not, according to their own discretion.

I've been guilty of giving advice to others that I do not follow myself—just like the State of Louisiana versus what it exacted from LPC. Although I do believe that if a piece of advice is worth my giving, it must be worth my following it, assuming the circumstances apply to both parties. The wisdom "always follow your own advice" sounds simple enough, but isn't easy to heed. Too many people advise the opposite: "Do as I say, not as I do," for the concept to be sustainable.

The lesson I glean from this is

Think first and then give advice with care.

MY ADVICE

The two sets of rules that I believed were in place—whether officially or unofficially—to regulate the practices of the State of Louisiana and also the United States government were disturbing to me on multiple levels. Rules are important to me, as are laws and regulations, and, for that matter, advice. Some might say I have a heightened sensitivity to and appreciation for rules and all that goes with them, and I might have to agree, but that is who I am and how I view the world. Evidence of how much I value brief rules and wise sayings comes in the form of the many professional reference and how-to books I buy and the seminars I elect to attend—all feature information summarized in concrete rules and sage advice.

You have no doubt noticed my affinity for summing up information in this book as "lessons," which are little more than brief statements of advice. Just as I like to receive advice and rules in the books and seminars I choose, I also like to create them. To do this, I analyze several different situations and find a general rule that helps me anticipate various predicaments.

A second reason why I make rules and give advice is to reduce the need for individuals to use their own judgment and discretion in business situations. Rules provide answers to frequently asked questions, eliminating the need for me or anyone else to ponder the same question each time it is asked, thereby saving the energy and time of all involved.

As a manager, I like to keep in close contact with the people I supervise. Two rules I have created for myself are, first, talk with every person I oversee for at least five minutes each day, and, second, meet with each person one-on-one for at least thirty minutes each week. Barring some kind of disaster, I follow these rules religiously because I'd rather address problems regularly throughout the course of a project than have them surprise me when it's potentially too late to make a correction.

While establishing rules and dispensing carefully thought-out advice at the onset of a project reduces the amount of "new thinking" I have to do each day, they cannot cover every situation. I have a meta-rule, a rule about my rules, to provide additional structure. My meta-rule asks the question, *"Does this rule fit this situation?"* If the answer is Yes, I apply the applicable rule and proceed. If the answer is No, I stop and devote some energy to thinking about the problem and identifying the best possible course of action.

Take My Advice, Please

When I make rules for and give advice to other people, I must be careful that what I offer fits the situation and that I can—and will—follow it myself. This can be somewhat tricky. I learned at the asphalt plant that I should follow my own advice, but I nevertheless sometimes find myself creating advice for others without much thought as to whether I would follow it myself.

There are a number of good reasons why I think other people should follow my advice. One is that I work for the government in government-contractor relations, and the government makes the rules. It's as simple as that. The government has the funding and makes the rules when it purchases systems from contractors. If a contractor wants government business, it will need to abide by the rules. The problem, of course, is that government employees are not always perfect rule-makers.

People generally do follow my advice, particularly when they know that, in many contracts, the government pays the contractor for *all work performed*—even for work that leads to an unsatisfactory product. The contractor follows the government's advice because it will be paid no matter what the result. If a contractor fights the government's advice, it may find the contract canceled. Given the choice, why not follow the government's advice?

Another situation in which people follow my advice occurs when I am their boss. The boss may not know everything, but the boss is the boss, and what the boss says goes. People either do as the boss decrees or they leave. This custom may not be the best system since the boss is not always correct. Sometimes, non-bosses need to help the boss to make better rules and to give more-sound advice.

The ego boost I feel when someone follows my advice can be dangerous (rules and regulations, of course, should be followed unless they are immoral or illegal, but advice is discretionary, bringing my ego to the fore). The danger is that I will fall into the trap of basing my self-esteem on how rigorously other people follow my advice.

Whether other people follow my advice is their choice, but if I feel happy when they follow it and unhappy when they choose otherwise, I am basing how I feel on what other people choose. I am giving them the power to influence my self-esteem and happiness for me, states that are too important to be decided by other people.

The best reason for people to follow my advice is because they know that I am right and that it is good advice. At times, however, people *pretend* they will follow my advice. They appear to accept it when standing in front of me, all the while knowing that their colleagues in the back office will do what they wanted to do all along. Perhaps they appear to accept my advice to appease me or to postpone conflict, but they don't like following it, will never like following it, and will not commit any resources to following it.

When people do not follow my advice, it may be because they are too busy working to listen to me. They may be so immersed in their problems that the building they work in could fall down around them and they wouldn't know it. This immersion-induced deafness occurs frequently, trust me, but the most costly episode I can recall occurred on a large project I worked on in the late 1990s.

With my coauthor Roy O'Bryan, I describe that project at length in *It Sounded Good When We Started*, the basic scenario being that a contractor building a system for the government was experiencing major problems that put it disastrously behind schedule and over budget. In an effort to recover, people were working ten- and twelve-hour days, six and seven days a week. I was the lead representative for the government team and I offered some advice that I believed would help people on the team, but they couldn't hear what I was saying. Their desire, drive, and professional pride—all qualities that I admire—prevented them from receiving advice that would help them succeed.

Sometimes, personal reasons prevent people from hearing and accepting my advice. When, for whatever reason, someone takes a dislike to me or feels defensive, my advice will fall on deaf ears. If a person doesn't respect me, say, because I am giving advice pertaining to what is his or her area of expertise and not mine, I might as well have been talking to the trees. The truth is, when I was young, I didn't let ignorance of a field prevent me from advising people. Much of my early advice fell on deaf ears, and it is good that it did.

Take My Advice, Say I to Myself

I *should* follow my own advice! To stay true to myself—to my integrity—I should act the same way regardless of the situation. This does not mean that I must do the same thing in every situation, but that I should exhibit the same values and attributes every day. If I expect other people to follow my advice, I should be a role model and do as I say.

Before giving advice, however, I need to be confident that it is complete and correct. By asking myself my meta-rule ("Does this rule fit this situation?"), I should catch poor advice before I air it—and I should find other rules that fit.

There are times when I don't follow my own advice because I don't want to, perhaps because I have grown bored with myself. I tend to do the same types of things every day at work and in my leisure time, and the routine can become oppressive and stifling. When following my own advice makes me stick to the same old routine in the same old haunts, I may choose to forget the past and jump at the chance to do something different. I should note, however, that these "follow a whim" occasions usually involve small stakes, so if forgetting my advice results in a whomping failure, the cost is small.

I also don't follow my own advice when it fails my first metarule and does not fit the situation. I haven't created advice for every conceivable situation, and I expect I never will. Life is all the more interesting because periodically I must handle situations that are exceptions to my rules.

Another time when I fail to follow my own advice occurs when I have—shame on me—forgotten exactly what it was I advocated. In a perfect universe populated by perfect people, this lapse should never be a danger, but my imperfect self has, on more than one occasion, planned what I was supposed to do and failed to do it. I had my advice to take, but I forgot it and failed. A case in point was a class I attended some years ago on how to run effective meetings. The importance of beginning every meeting by appointing one person to record the official minutes had been hammered into us each day, but when it was my turn to preside over a practice meeting, I forgot the rule. Halfway through the meeting, I had a flash—I had forgotten to appoint anyone to take notes. I jumped up out of my chair, pointed to the person to my immediate right, and shouted, *"You! You take the notes for this meeting!"*

That was not my finest moment as I had certainly forgotten to take my own advice of following the rules, but I was in training to be a leader and a manager, so perhaps I can be forgiven. Worse is when I, now, as a manager, must manipulate or abandon my own advice because it is off-center emotionally and not worth following. When I am cool, calm, and collected, I am centered. When I am angry, afraid, nervous, stressed, or tired, I am not centered. My emotions, like everyone else's, can run in wild directions.

Wild-running emotions are not the big problem, however. How I react to them is the crucial element because, when my emotions threaten to run wild, I fall into the trap of concentrating on finding some enemy external to myself. My mind is racing somewhere, fighting battles against imaginary foes. As a result, I cannot remember much of anything, which brings me to my second meta-rule: *"In order to remember rules, be centered."*

Being centered does not mean chasing away emotions. My emotions provide information, and I need to use that information. Being centered means dealing with my emotions in a positive manner. I did not do this successfully some years ago when I received an e-mail at work from a colleague who didn't like the feedback I'd noted on a document he'd written. Reading his e-mail, I became quite emotional: How dare he question my motives? Who does he think he is to suggest I didn't know what I was talking about by providing feedback as I did?

In this case, I was able to think about the emotions I was feeling before I needed to interact with the person who had sent the e-mail. I realized that I was upset because he was chastising me. Adults chastise children, and I was not a child. That was it! I was not a child; I did not need to be frightened like a child; I did not need to react in a childish manner. Instead, I could react like a mature adult by being centered and following my own advice for such situations. I remembered my own advice, applied my meta-rules, and worked through the situation with this colleague in a manner that helped both of us.

ADVICE FOR MY ADVICE

I've learned the hard way about giving advice as a manager. Before giving advice to others, I work with it over time. First, I write the advice on paper with a pencil. This act helps commit the advice to my memory. Once the advice is written on paper and is embedded in my mind, I experiment with the validity of the advice. I think of cases in which the advice would work, and then I jot a shorthand version of each of those case names on the left side of my piece of paper. Then, I think of cases in which the advice would not work, and note those cases on the right side of the same piece of paper.

Once I have processed all facets of the advice for a while, I practice giving it. Since this advice is still experimental, I try it out in situations that are neither project- nor life-critical. I may preface my advice-giving experiment by telling people, "I'm not sure about this situation. I've been thinking about things like this and I have an idea that we might try. I'm not sure if it will work, but we have the situation well enough under control that we can recover if it doesn't."

After the session, I write the results of the advice-giving experiment on my original sheet of paper. When I offer advice, I take care in how I give it. I make sure to speak for myself. I introduce my advice with something like the following: "I am usually better at supervising a team when I can speak with everyone on the team for five or ten minutes every day. I encourage you to try this." Explaining my approach with words that reveal my role seems to work much better for me than removing myself from the advice, saying, for example, "They say that good supervisors speak with everyone five minutes every day."

Wording my advice as I worded it in the first example above also carries weight because I can speak from experience. I am stating that when I take time to speak with each person I supervise for some time each day, I am a better supervisor. I am saying, "I have practiced this, and it is my personal experience, not just theory." I am also speaking in realistic versus idealistic terms, communicating to people that I am sincere in wanting to be the best supervisor I can be. I don't claim that holding daily five-minute meetings with each person will result in my being a better supervisor, but I feel the strategy is worth the try. The technique *seems* to make me a "better" supervisor, but I don't claim that it will make me a great or even a good supervisor.

CONCLUSIONS

I didn't think much about culture while I was working at the asphalt plant. At age eighteen, when I started working at the plant, I thought that culture meant going to a symphony to hear classical music or to a massive library to absorb stored knowledge amassed over the ages. Shoveling rocks could have nothing to do with culture, I thought. Well, I was wrong. The culture I absorbed at the asphalt plant was the culture of working men, the culture of different generations, and the culture of government-industry "cooperation."

I remember the first time I saw a State of Louisiana dump truck pull out in the rain with its load of asphalt open to the sky. The steam shot up from the truck bed, and I could imagine a layer of hard crust forming on top of the asphalt. I looked around to someone in the control room where I was working, and said, "Hey, they're not covering their load."

The reply was calm and matter of fact: "That's a State truck. State workers don't cover their loads."

I winced. That didn't make sense. What they were doing was negligent, and, equally important to me, it wasn't fair. The concept of fairness has always held me in its grip, and this practice flouted that concept. In all the years I have been in business, I have advised myself not to worry so much about fairness—life isn't fair, people aren't fair, so don't expect business to be fair—but I continue to worry about fairness in different cultures.

The most valuable lessons I gathered from witnessing different cultures are

A different culture can reveal a new set of possibilities.

Think first and then give advice with care.

REFERENCES

[OBR04]   R. O'Bryan and D. Phillips, *It Sounded Good When We Started: A Project Manager's Guide to Working With People on Projects* (New York: IEEE Computer Society Press/John Wiley and Sons, 2004).

SIX

Risk and Opportunity

I like certainty in the projects I manage, but expecting it isn't realistic. Improbable events happen on projects. Many bring about damaging consequences, but others result in good. As a manager, I should be ready for the improbable. Fortunately, I have learned, and developed an arsenal of, techniques and practices to help me be prepared as a manager—for risks as well as opportunities. Sometimes, these are one and the same.

I took part in a different culture at the asphalt plant. The workers at Louisiana Paving were an interesting group of people from whom I learned a tremendous amount. One of the most amazing things I witnessed was people bending steel bars. That's right— people bending steel bars. I was quite surprised as I'd been fairly certain up to that point that only Superman could bend steel bars.

Throughout my career, I have continued to see improbable events that were beneficial to the workplace. I have been troubled, however, by the fact that most of the time, we weren't ready to take advantage of these good surprises. Sometimes, we lost opportunities and poor results followed.

I don't usually enjoy surprising events in connection with a project. I study, think ahead, and plan. Things should work out according to my plans. Unplanned factors, however, seem to sneak in as if chance played a part in projects and life.

Chance, as a part of life and work, is not new. It has been reckoned with for so long that it is a field of scientific study. Improbable but good events happen; improbable but bad events happen.

These events can be put into numbers and equations, a fact that I find comfort in.

Remaining flexible no matter what happens is one of the most valuable secrets of management I know. The first step to ensuring flexibility is to know your own limits, but opportunity and risk also must be factored into the equation.

BENDING METAL

While doing repair work on the conveyor belts and other moving parts of the asphalt plant, we usually would need to move large, heavy objects from one location to another so that we could access the part needing repair. We used a front-end loader or other piece of machinery for the job whenever we could get it close enough to the object to move it. When we couldn't get close, we used brute-strength muscle, some brains, and a pry bar.

The pry bar was made of steel, about three inches in diameter and about eight-feet long. Sometimes, we positioned the pry bar against an object to keep the object from shifting position while we worked behind it or beside it on whatever needed repair. Other times, we put the pry bar under the object and pushed, using the pry bar as a lever.

There were times when we tried to move an object using the pry bar as a lever, but the object would not move. Two or three of us would lean into the pry bar and push against the object with all our weight and strength. If the object still wouldn't budge, we'd move out of the way and call for one of the plant's two strongest men to come over and push by himself. It turned out that one really strong man could push harder than two or three of the rest of us, by getting into what the crew bosses called "the optimum position to push."

There were two men at the plant who were especially strong. Jackson was one of them, and he would climb down from his front-end loader and position his 300-pounds-plus frame against the object and strain against it until it budged. The other strong man was Otis, who weighed about the same as Jackson but, at eight inches taller, didn't have the girth.

Either Otis or Jackson would be called into service when two or three regular laborers using the pry bar weren't strong enough to move the object, but there were times when even one or the other of these strongest men would lean into the object and manipulate the pry bar lever, but the object would not move. Otis or Jackson would lean into the bar again and again with still no movement. By this time, the pry bar would begin to bend. Until I saw it happen the first time, I didn't think a three-inch-diameter steel bar could bend.

Maybe the pry bars weren't actually solid steel; maybe they had a good portion of soft metal blended with the steel, but whatever the case, I was surprised to see them bend. They never bent when two or three laborers leaned into them, but here were two big, middle-aged men, wearing work clothes just like the rest of us, struggling to keep their footing in loose gravel, bending metal bars.

I learned by seeing it with my own eyes that

The strongest things can bend.

RISKY BUSINESS

Business—not to mention life—requires navigation through the uncertain and the unknown. That the pry bar would actually bend was an improbable but good outcome, because the fact of the bar bending served as a pressure valve to tell Otis or Jackson to stop pushing before someone got hurt or something snapped. The outcome was also good for me, because seeing steel bend showed me that things that I thought could not happen sometimes do happen.

Improbable things still happen to me, which can be very disturbing to me as I am not always ready to reap the benefits. One such event occurred in early 2001 when I was a speaker at the Software Management Conference in San Diego. I was thrilled to be invited, but I did not expect to have much attention from the attendees as I'd never before spoken at a conference and I was not known in the field. At the appointed time, I stood on a large stage and addressed about one hundred people in an auditorium that could easily have held one thousand. I was nervous at first, but when I relaxed, the audience paid attention to what I was saying. The talk went well and, overall, it was a very good experience.

What happened afterwards was a pleasant surprise. People came up to me at the podium when I finished speaking to ask questions about my topic. Other members of the audience came up to ask questions—*about me.* "Are you a consultant?" "Could you visit our company to consult?" "Could you visit our local chapter to give your talk again?" "Could I have your business card?"

I was surprised—maybe as astonished as when I saw Jackson bend the pry bar. I wasn't ready for affirmation and invitation, but what I was least prepared for were the requests for my business card. I am a government employee, and very few government employees have business cards. If I had anticipated the requests, I could have gone to my local copy shop to create some personal cards bearing my name and contact information. But I didn't expect such success at the conference, and I wasn't ready for it.

Later in the week, a magazine editor interviewed me about my topic and asked whether I would be willing to write a short piece for his magazine. When the editor asked for my business card, I grinned with embarrassment, and then I promised to mail one off once I'd gotten back home—I didn't mention that I would need to get cards printed first.

Not being prepared for the improbable can be potentially life-threatening. Early in my engineering career, I dealt directly with a company that would go out of business because an improbable event occurred and the company was not ready to reap the benefits. The company made a small radio that the Defense Department used a dozen or so of each year.

The snowball started growing when we started a major project for which a hundred of these radios were needed. The order seemed a great thing for the company, increasing its sales one-thousand percent in one day. What an improbable event!

The company, however, was not prepared for this opportunity. It was a very small company with only three or four employees who worked full-time to order the parts and to assemble the radios. It didn't have enough people to fill the large order we had placed, but it seemed that all it needed to do was hire people. There were qualified people available to hire, but this little company didn't have anyone who knew how to interview and hire— they all were engineers and technicians who did technical work.

And so, without adding any staff, they set out to build our one-hundred radios.

Besides the difference in scale between the task of ordering and assembling parts for twelve radios in a year versus one-hundred radios for delivery in six months, the little company wasn't prepared for the fact that the customer who anticipates delivery of a large, important order within this timeframe wants to know, on a weekly basis, how the work is progressing.   As time marches on, pressure builds.

We were accustomed to purchasing one-hundred units of product on a single order, and so we proceeded as we always did: After the first few weeks, we called the company a couple of times a week to monitor the status of our order. When no one answered our phone calls (they later explained that they couldn't take time for phone calls because they were too busy trying to gather parts and assemble our radios), we called them again and again, to no avail. Our next step was to visit them to meet face-to-face. They told us that they were working hard and were making progress, but asked us to stay away as the meetings were taking them away from building radios. They admitted that they were behind schedule.

They promised to work longer hours each day to catch up. With twelve-hour days, seven days a week, productivity increased, but the long hours wore on them. Fatigue led to nagging illnesses that meant missed days of work. As they had never experienced this type of sickness and had not planned for lost days, they again fell behind schedule.

To compensate, they tried harder, but fatigue and sickness led to mistakes. In the past, they had had to do very little rework building each radio because they took their time and made few mistakes. Now they were hurrying, fatigued, and sick, and they found many problems when they ran final tests on the few radios they had managed to produce in the time since receiving our order. Finding and fixing the problems led to additional time lost.

Faced with inferior and defective product, the company had nothing to deliver. No deliveries meant no payments; no payments meant no new income for the company. It had drained its resources and depleted its financial reserves buying parts and paying salaries and sick pay. With no new income coming in, the company could no longer pay the employees and, within a fairly short period of time, sold its radio design to a competitor and closed its doors.

Within the year, the second company had manufactured enough high-performance, small radios to deliver our hundred-unit order. The little company going out of business was a depressing and seemingly improbable event, but the big company was prepared to take advantage of an opportunity, and we eventually got what we had ordered. It was not a happy scenario, but it taught me a valuable lesson.

HALF EMPTY OR HALF FULL?

Things that seem improbable can happen, and sometimes, what happens *is* for the good. Preparing for the improbable does not require one to be an optimist or a pessimist, but rather, a realist. Consider the time that I spoke at the conference. Before the conference, I might have foreseen several possible outcomes. One was that my talk would be a failure, I would not make any contact with the audience, I would forget what I wanted to say, and I would stumble through the longest hour of my life.

Another possible outcome was that my talk would be a success and would lead to my getting a considerable amount of future work as a conference speaker, consultant, and writer, much like what actually happened. The third possible outcome was that the talk would be fine, but that it would not lead to any future business for me as a speaker, a consultant, or an author. This third outcome seemed the most probable, and so I prepared only for the probable.

I wasn't being realistic when I went to San Diego ready for the probable yet unprepared for the improbable. I knew that the *chance* of a good outcome was greater than zero, but I nevertheless treated the chance as being zero. I didn't consider for a moment what might be possible if the outcome were good. Hence, I didn't take the half hour needed to print up some business cards with personal contact information to give to people if asked to do so.

I have difficulty looking forward to a good but improbable outcome. There is something in my temperament that leads me to believe that improbably bad outcomes are far more probable than improbably good outcomes. Old adages such as "Don't count your chickens before they hatch," and "Save your pennies for a rainy day" are burned in my mind.

Part of the reason for my prudence and pessimism comes from my father. He knew men who saved and prepared for retirement, only to die a short time after retiring. I would argue that they had prepared for a good but improbable outcome, further noting that because most people retire at an age when their own health or the health of their spouse or life-partner either is failing or is likely to soon fail, they face unanticipated hardships, making an enjoyable retirement improbable. Tragically, my father was saving and preparing for an enjoyable retirement when he was killed in an automobile accident three years before his retirement was to begin, further reinforcing views held by my pessimistic inner self.

I do believe it is realistic to prepare for improbably good outcomes, however. Lost opportunities are lost, and there are few, if any, chances to have at them again, so being prepared both for the probable and the improbable is wise.

Chance—and Risk—at Work

As manager, I can hope for and against certain chances, and I can plan to avoid certain risks. I plan budgets, activities, training schedules, and technological maturity. One aspect of planning is making estimates. Managers estimate how much time, money, and manpower a task requires. As hard as we try, these estimates are guesses. They may be educated guesses, reviewed guesses, or second guesses, but they are still guesses. When managers guess at a future event, there are different possible outcomes—some of which are good, some bad, and some in a comfortable middle.

Nothing appeals to me more than knowing for sure that a project will succeed. I like this so much that I spend extra time planning. I work through my estimates multiple times and then I share these with other people to learn their opinions. I use models for estimating and adjust my models after the project finishes so that I will estimate better the next time.

Some of this may sound foreign to readers who would rather plunge into a project with more spontaneity and unknowns than I ever would permit. I have worked with people like you. I understand how you feel, but I don't share the way you do things.

Regardless of our differences, I believe that we two types—planners and wingers—share one thing in common. We both like to have power over our projects. Many non-planners have told me, "Detailed planning won't ever take the place of smart people working hard."

Adherents of agile development in the software field take this view, emphasizing process in lieu of detailed planning, and preferring short bursts of intense work interspersed with breaks during which to reassess project progress. They put their trust in hard work, smart decisions, and collaboration—all resources that provide power over projects—to bring a project to successful conclusion.

The *power of people* in projects is the best resource I can use to combat risk and to prepare against bad outcomes—I avoid projects where I don't have people on board who know what they are doing and who want to do their best job—but there is also a place in projects for *chance.* Managers can strengthen a project and make it more likely to succeed when they can face and overcome risk, but such a project is still vulnerable to chance because there are things outside of anyone's control that can affect project outcome. For example, the economy as a whole can change the job market, causing a swing in the unemployment rate that can hinder the hiring of needed people. The project manager in such a situation did nothing to cause that change in unemployment and can do nothing to reverse it. It is a break that is outside his or her control.

I have experienced the influence of chance at different times in my career. When I was writing software at the digital signal-processing lab in the early 1990s, several of us saw the great promise of a supercomputer for the processing we were doing. I was committed to porting software to the supercomputer and spreading its benefits to as many users as I could. The technical and business merits of this approach were obvious to me, but I didn't know whether I could convince my colleagues.

Chance fell my way with an improbable but good outcome. Our management had contracted with an outstandingly qualified engineering firm to build a special-purpose, high-speed, processing system, and my organization had allocated $18 million to the engineering firm to build the system. The firm was doing everything right—from requirements analysis and design to implementation and reviews. It had experts on hand from its own staff as well as a group of consultants who also were experts in the area. They did everything right, but they failed to build the special-purpose, high-speed, processing system that would do what we needed.

Their eventual failure was all chance for me. On the heels of the disaster, and just as my management was searching for an alternative to the spec-ed processing system, I happened to be sitting by, committed to preaching the virtues of porting software to a supercomputer processing system. With the help of a team of really capable people, we put the right software on a supercomputer within a few months, using an approach that yielded a processing capability that was far better and far cheaper than the engineering firm had tried to build.

I have also had chance turn against me. At another point during the early 1990s, I wrote a book on image processing. The published book had some success selling in a small market, but I worried about some notable shortcomings in the book and in the software I had written to go along with the book. I decided to upgrade the book for a second edition, working hard to rewrite most of the software and altering the text to describe the revised software.

The revised text and software for the second edition were good, and I was elated to turn over this vastly improved material to my editor, who was eager to publish the second edition. But something happened that dramatically changed the course of events: Just before I delivered material to my editor, my publisher was bought by a larger company whose management planned to take it in a different direction. Neither I nor my editor had any inkling of the pending sale in advance of the purchase. It just happened by chance that there would be no second edition.

Frustrated but not completely thwarted, I still hoped to publish the second edition. I search for and found an online marketer of electronic books that showed interest in putting a softcopy version of my book on its Website, with a plan to sell electronic versions of it. That seemed like a great solution. My second edition would be available online for purchase.

Chance, however, fell the other way and produced a bad outcome for me. The venture into electronic publishing did not pan out as initially expected. It seemed that most people really didn't want to purchase this type of book online and download it. Most readers seemed to want old-fashioned, print-on-paper books to hold in their hands and read. I had no way to influence their desire. It was all chance that produced a bad outcome for me.

BEING READY FOR GOOD OUTCOMES

I work hard and use my mind, and I do what I can to ensure that my colleagues do the same. To make the most of our efforts, I must be ready to take advantage of opportunities and good outcomes.

I plan projects in terms of *should do, could do,* and *would do.* When I plan *should-do* things, I list necessary steps such as,

1) talk with the user,
2) analyze the requirements,
3) design several solutions,
4) implement the one I think is best, and
5) test.

Next, I look for the things I could do to get more time for essential tasks. I begin the process by asking "what if" questions. For example, "What if I shorten the analysis phase?" "What if I focus on testing instead of coding?" "What if I spend less time with the user and more time with my team?" After each question, I ask the *could-do* question: "What could I do with that extra time?"

Finally, I try to consider what I *would do* to react to risk or opportunity situations. I ask myself, "What would I do if . . . ?" For example, "What would I do if no one on my team is seriously ill this year?" "What would I do with the team if we finish this project a month early?" "What would I do if the price of computers drops below X?" "What would I do if our chief engineer makes a breakthrough in algorithm development and we only need half the memory we estimated?"

Thinking through would-do questions helps me explore opportunities and make plans. I wish that before I set off for that first conference in San Diego, I had asked myself, "What would I do if people love my speech and want me to repeat it in front of people at their company?" The radio company could have asked, "What would we do if our sales jumped some order of magnitude, say, by one-hundred or even one-thousand percent?"

One decades-old but still effective way to phrase would-do questions is by using the Program Evaluation and Review Technique (PERT). A technique that helps people plan projects, PERT utilizes a network of rectangles connected by arrows leading from one rectangle to another. Each rectangle represents a task, and the directed arrows show how one task leads to another. The information inside each rectangle describes one task as well as the resources needed to complete it.

One extremely important resource to note on a PERT chart is *time*—the length of time each task is expected to take can be noted with three estimated durations: worst case, expected case, and best case. A true PERT chart allows a planner to calculate the length of a project if everything goes poorly, goes as expected, or goes remarkably well. PERT also allows for limitless combinations of these cases. Most planners only project the expected length of a task, a practice that invites risk into a project.

PERT helps planners plan for good outcomes by encouraging them to consider what would happen if everything goes well on a project—for an improbable but good outcome. I don't recall ever having a project where everything went perfectly, but I have experienced an entire phase of a project going well. With PERT, I can modify my plans to incorporate success and setbacks into the overall project.

Thoughts on Bending Metal

Whenever I see something bend that I did not expect would have flexibility, I think back to the bending pry bar at the asphalt plant. My amazement at seeing the pry bar bend caused me to notice other things that bend. For example, lumber used in construction bends, stretches, and shrinks. Antenna towers that stretch up one-hundred feet in height sometimes bend past the point at which they should snap in two, and then they straighten back to their original shape.

It may seem strange, but things that bend are often stronger than things that don't. The bend—and accompanying rebound—is evidence of remarkable strength in an otherwise ordinary object, but the force bending the object also must be credited with having great strength. I admired what Jackson and Otis could do in bending the pry bars, but I also have respect for the bars themselves because I have never come close to bending a steel bar.

The bending pry bar has also helped me observe resilience in people. I have seen some people work to exhaustion, and, after only a few minutes of rest, again be ready to work. I noticed how my mother was resilient in dealing with the sudden and devastating death of my father. She never resembled a steel bar much before that day, but she has often since. My ability to observe and appreciate things that shouldn't bend, but do, came from knowing Jackson and Otis and watching them do the improbable.

Holding Onto Chains

At the asphalt plant, whenever we needed to move large, heavy objects, we used a front-end loader that the men souped up with a homemade crane they had made by attaching two pipes to the front-end loader's bucket in such a way as to form a triangle, pointing outward. This triangle arrangement formed a boom that they connected by a long, heavy chain to the top of the loader's bucket. It had a large, steel hook that hung down from the apex of the triangle, to which we could secure a second chain around the object we wanted to move, and then connect the end of this chain to the steel hook.

The chain that we wrapped around the object to be moved was made of large, thick, steel links of half-inch- or three-quarters-inch-diameter steel, about the thickness of my index finger. This homemade crane may sound flimsy, but the contraption worked quite well.

When I was first working at the asphalt plant, my job usually was to place my hand on the side of whatever we were lifting to guide it and keep it from swinging. At first, I held onto the chain itself until the experienced men stopped me from doing that. They explained that if the chain broke, so would my hand, arm, and half the bones in my body.

I never actually saw one of these chains break and, given their construction, I didn't really believe they could break, but the looks on the men's faces convinced me to never put my hand or any other part of me on something we were lifting with the crane.

Their stories taught me to believe that

The strongest things can break.

FACING RISK

I have stumbled through many risk-infused venues in my career. Some I knew about ahead of time, while others didn't even cross my mind because I didn't think anything could possibly go wrong.

An improbable but bad situation arose when my organization outsourced to an engineering company in the late 1990s. I've mentioned the project in previous chapters and at length in *It Sounded Good When We Started*, but in this particular situation, our prime contractor sub-contracted the building of some circuit boards, which were to be built to unusually close tolerances. Such tolerances were rare, but they had been accomplished before. Our prime contractor hired a qualified sub-contractor, but six weeks later, the sub-contractor's rep called with the bad news: It had tried many times to make the circuit boards, but could not meet the tolerances. The rep said the company was taking itself off the contract.

Our prime contractor searched for and hired a second qualified sub-contractor. Five weeks later, the second sub-contractor called and stated that it could not meet the tolerances either, so it also quit. We were frustrated, especially since at this point, the prime contractor was spending $40,000 a day on salaries for engineers and assemblers, money that was completely going to waste while they were waiting for the circuit boards.

Because the sub-contract was budgeted for only $20,000, we encouraged the prime contractor to hire two or three sub-contractors to work simultaneously, in the hope that surely one of them would succeed. The prime contractor argued that it was a waste of money to pay three qualified sub-contractors to do the same work at the same time. We replied that no matter how improbable it seemed that the next qualified sub-contractor also would fail to produce the circuit boards, it was still possible, resulting in another five or six weeks during which the combined force of engineers and assemblers would take home another $40,000 each day. Since the circuit boards only cost one-half day's spending, hiring several sub-contractors was a good hedge against an improbable but bad outcome.

The prime contractor did not heed our advice and did not use multiple sub-contractors. It hired one qualified sub-contractor after another, and one qualified sub-contractor after another failed. The prime contractor finally found a crew that could deliver, but only after the project had lost valuable time and had wasted disgusting amounts of money.

In this story, I use the term "qualified" many times. I do so to emphasize that the prime contractor did the necessary research and hired sub-contractors that should have been able to deliver. The failure of the sub-contractors was improbable, but the chance of failure was greater than zero. The prime contractor, however, acted as if the chance of failure was zero.

SOME THINGS ARE TOUGH

In addition to chance, the element of difficulty plays a role in bad outcomes. I've participated in dozens of projects during my career. In most of those, we were trying to build something that didn't exist. Building things that don't already exist is usually tough. If it were easy, someone would have already built the thing, and then it would exist now.

In spite of problems that can be caused by chance and difficulty, I've always gone into projects expecting to succeed, even when I was a young manager. I suppose I was overconfident, but overconfidence seems to be common among managers, especially young ones.

Overconfidence could explain why some improbable but bad outcomes have occurred on some of the projects I had expected would succeed, although it is possible that the bad outcome wasn't improbable; possibly it was my estimation of probability that was wrong. When creating something that doesn't exist, I need to remember that bad outcomes are probable instead of improbable. The reason being that chance, difficulty, and overconfidence all play a role.

SOME PEOPLE AREN'T SO TOUGH

We've seen how things made out of steel and other strong materials can bend and, sometimes, even break, but a manager needs to be alert to the fact that people can break, too. People break in ways that are different from the ways steel or glass or wire break, however. Some people suddenly snap, having tolerated an intolerable condition for too long.

I worked with a man who had fought the daily commuting battle for a decade or more, driving between his job in the District of Columbia, and his suburban Virginia home. One stiflingly hot August day, stuck in a particularly tiresome traffic jam, he snapped, resolving to call a recruiter he knew who had told him about a job close to his home. As soon as he arrived at work, he called the recruiter to tell him he would take the job. He then hung up the phone, walked into his supervisor's office to quit, and climbed right back into his car to drive back to Virginia to his new job.

He had snapped that hot August day and made a hasty decision that he would come to regret, suffering for several years through work he didn't enjoy. He thought long and hard before changing jobs again, but eventually he returned to commuting—through even more horrendous traffic than he'd previously experienced—because it was back to a job that he truly loved doing. He now understood the tradeoffs and accepted the arduous commute.

At the signal-processing lab, one of the men plumb disappeared: He was at work one day and not at work thereafter. Months later, we learned that although he'd always seemed to do his job competently and in a quiet and unassuming manner, he'd had a drinking problem. Something happened on what turned out to be his last day on the job that caused him to break down and drink himself out of a job.

I, too, almost "broke" at the signal-processing lab. I was working hard, and I believed that I was performing my job well above the undeniably high standards set for us—but I was frustrated, angry, and demoralized by the way the old-timers in command treated me, offering neither appreciations nor promotions in acknowledgment of my work's contribution to the lab's bottom line. The turning point came when my wife confronted me, pointing out how I was directing my frustration and anger at her and at our three young sons. She told me bluntly that I needed to change something—either the job or how I acted at home because of the job.

I am eternally thankful my wife caught me before I broke. As a result of Karen's and our boys' patience, love, and understanding, I learned to ignore most of what was happening around me at work, made it through the experience—with my marriage and family intact—and eventually moved on to other jobs.

One of the most traumatic days in my young life occurred in high school when a classmate "broke" and hung himself. He did not leave a suicide note, but we learned after he died that he'd been extremely depressed, presumably because his sister, who was blind, needed more and more attention at home, putting an unbearable strain on everyone in the family. Rather than carry on, tragically, he broke.

This section has been depressing to write and it undoubtedly has been depressing to read, but I've included it because I want fellow managers to understand how tragic it is when people break. Most people appear to be strong and resilient, but appearances can be deceiving. People can suddenly quit their job, fall into alcoholism, ruin their family life, or hang themselves—because of things beyond their control.

Objects also are not as perfect and strong as they might appear. I need to be careful not to load an object in such a way that breaks a steel chain. I need to be careful not to say something that breaks a person.

The most difficult task for a manager is to notice when someone snaps or breaks. People don't usually break right in front of everyone at work. They may break on the inside while at work, but the breakage doesn't manifest itself then and there. They stay at their desk for the rest of the day, leave work, and then break later, alone.

To prevent even small breaks from happening, managers must train themselves to notice when an event happens or something is said that could break a person on the inside. The best way I've found to increase my sensitivity to potential breakage is to observe and listen to what goes on around me. As long as I keep in mind the fact that people and things *do* break, and I keep my eyes and ears open, I will be performing this part of my job as manager as well as I can.

RISK MANAGEMENT

All is not hopeless for managers—risk has been with us for centuries, and managers have developed techniques for dealing with it. The field of risk management is devoted to managing those improbable but bad outcomes *(for strategies on modern risk management, see* [DEM03]). I follow five steps that help me to manage risk: Identify, plan, set triggers, observe, and act.

Identify

The first step I take is to ask a very big question: "What could possibly go wrong?" The answer to this question helps me identify risks or potential problems. To answer, I must acknowledge that I can be overconfident at times and that my plans are not always perfect. Although I don't like to admit that my plans sometimes fail, my experience with many potential problems becoming real problems has made it easier to acknowledge.

To get started, I consider what seem to be my favorite three categories of potential problems: *people, process,* and *product.* I start with product and end with people, the idea being to save the most important for last.

Technical hype is a potential problem related to product. Businesses advertise that their product does just about everything better than every other product that came before it. People believe the hype and plan projects based on it. When the product doesn't live up to the hype, the project may be at risk.

Process—what work is to be done in what order—is susceptible to myriad problems. The process for one project might be to plan the complete project in excruciating but necessary detail before beginning any work. Process for another project could be to plan the first week's work, and then to perform the work for that week; next, plan the work for the second week and then do that week's work; and so on. Neither of these processes is going to be the best approach to use in every situation, and so it is up to the manager to pick what process is best for the project at hand.

Earlier, I wrote about the engineering firm that failed to deliver a new signal-processing system to our lab. The firm was hired on the assumption that it would be able to invent a new system to solve a problem the lab had been unable to solve. Its managers chose a process that, first, took all the known requirements into consideration; second, designed a system in detail from first phase through delivery; third, built the system; and fourth, tested the system. This formal process, which the firm elected to follow, required the staff to complete work on one step prior to proceeding to the next step. Experimentation and looking ahead to the next step were not permitted.

This four-step sequential process was, it turned out, the wrong approach for that project. Inventing the unknown requires trying some experiments and even some diversionary trips down the wrong paths. People on the project were smart and worked hard, but they could not overcome the limitations of the process their managers elected to follow.

As with process and product, there is risk associated with the very people a manager chooses to staff a project. People live real lives, taking vacations, becoming ill, losing interest in their job, quitting, and, in the worst-case scenario, sometimes even dying during the course of a project.

Simply by having a personal life, one person single-handedly can sidetrack or derail even the best-laid plans. When people's emotions come into the picture, planning truly must take a back seat. We've all had days when we're in a very good mood, feeling upbeat and capable of conquering all challenges. On such days, we find that we can work wonders. And we've all also had days when a bad mood and bad karma and bad timing prevent us from accomplishing much of anything. As a manager, I should not (and usually cannot) create or control my people's good and bad moods; they usually happen on their own. I can strive to control my own moods to make the most of opportunities as they present themselves, however, and by identifying potential problems and planning how to cope if they materialize, I can manage the risk that people's personal lives bring to my project.

One reason seeing people as a source of risk seems to be overlooked by most managers is that we tend to see our staff and colleagues as some kind of superhuman beings—not made of flesh and blood, but bionic. As such, we expect them to come to work day after day without interruption. Whatever product or process problem comes their way, they will solve it. They will enjoy performing these great feats, doing them all just for their manager. This viewpoint is, of course, based in fantasy, not reality. People are human—not superhuman.

Plan

Once I answer the question, "What could possibly go wrong?" I need *a plan* to manage the potential problems I've identified. I now consider the question, "If Plan A doesn't work, what will I do?" I will create Plan B.

To prepare myself, I try to imagine the project hitting a snag that will make it necessary for me to change course by changing the work itself or by changing the process for doing the work. To change the work, I will need to identify a different set of resources, such as other methodologies, other specialists, or other hardware and software. As soon as I have identified my Plan B resources, I should take steps to ensure they can be available if I need them. For example, I should list the people I will need, and then start contacting them to confirm their availability. At this point, I don't know whether I will need them, but I do know I *may* need them.

The importance of knowing what you'll do as Plan B *before the improbable occurs* is a lesson I learned at the asphalt plant when I saw one of the plant's more experienced mechanics pull the Buck folding knife from my fellow laborer's leather waist-pouch in order to slash the conveyor belt and stop its movement—all in time to save the laborer's fingers from the certainty of being crushed or amputated. That mechanic's quick thinking was evidence of his Plan B, put into play when our Plan A (to reverse or stop the belt's movement) was not working. Clearly, the mechanic had seen this type of problem before, and he had also seen the solution before.

Set Triggers

At this point, I already should have identified the improbable and bad events that might occur, assessed the risk, and devised my *best* Plan B to handle such events. My next step is to *set triggers.* These will be set in locations that answer the question, "When should I stop Plan A and switch to Plan B?"

Developing the new system at the signal-processing lab, we needed a Plan B when progress with Plan A stopped dead in its tracks. We'd been ahead of schedule for the first three weeks, but then we stalled. We tried a few things to prime progress, but our stall continued until we hit a dead stop, at which point I brought in the vendor whose efforts also failed. I worked on the problem myself after the vendor made no progress.

This activity all sounds well planned and executed, but I have to admit that I didn't think far enough ahead at the time to have "a plan" documented. I do recall having triggers in my mind, if not on paper. My thinking went like this: *If Team A doesn't solve the problem in a week, bring in Team B; if Team B doesn't solve the problem in another week, do something else.* These triggers helped me manage the situation.

Observe

So far in this discussion of risk management, I have identified potential problems, planned ways to work around the problems, and set triggers to remind myself when to implement Plan B. At this point, it is time to *observe*, which, in this case, means gathering status on the project. I again recommend looking at people, product, and process, as the primary sources of risk.

As I gather information regarding project status, I need to take care to verify the accuracy of what I observe. Problems in the project mean I made a mistake in planning. That can be hard to accept, no matter how clearly the status indicates mistakes have been made. I recommend checking the status twice to be sure of its implications. Then, I need to accept and believe in what the status tells me.

Act

Now it is time to do what I am actually most expected (and paid!) to do—manage the work in light of the changed circumstances. So, the first thing I do is face up to the fact that an improbable event has occurred. I am ready because I have already identified that this particular event, although improbable, could occur. I planned for it; I set a trigger to indicate it has occurred; and I gathered details about the status for the project. It would seem that my act of managing—making the switch from Plan A to Plan B—should be easy. All I need to do is give the word and my people, *immediately and seamlessly,* will go in a different direction. Right!

This step can be the most difficult. One reason for the difficulty is that self-esteem often comes into the picture at this point. Imagine this scenario: The work is going poorly; I am the manager; I am responsible for the work; I have failed somewhere. For many reasons, failure doesn't sit well with me, but one of the major reasons it doesn't sit well is that it causes me to question my ability to do *anything* right. My thinking at such a time goes like this: *"If I made mistakes managing the work currently being done on the project, I might also be mistaken in what I've envisioned for Plan B. Maybe if I wait a while longer, the facts might change to show that Plan A was right all along."* Whenever I have any doubt as to whether what I am doing is the optimal strategy, I tend to freeze up. I need to pay special attention so as not to let my doubt lead to low self-esteem and a kind of work-related mental paralysis.

When project status information indicates that I should take action and switch to Plan B, I have arrived at a crucial point, a moment of truth, as a manager. I need to remind myself that when I worked through the risk-management steps before the project began, I was calm, breathing normally, and thinking clearly. If I am not calm and thinking clearly now that the work appears to be spiraling out of control and off-course, I need to follow the risk-management fundamentals and implement Plan B.

Thoughts on Holding Onto Chains

I don't think I ever saw a chain break at the asphalt plant, and I certainly never witnessed a significant accident during my four years working there, but accidents did occur. I worked alongside one man who had had his foot crushed by a twenty-ton roller while working on a road crew. It happened a few years before I joined the company.

The most terrible accident that happened to anyone on the plant's payroll was the one that claimed my father's life ten years after I left the company. My dad was driving his company pickup truck around a sharp curve and was met head-on by a semi-trailer that crossed over into his lane.

My father's death was an improbable and devastating tragedy for which no amount of risk-management planning could have prepared anyone at the plant, and it certainly was cause for the greatest and saddest shock my mother, two brothers, and I were ever called on to face. It seems, however, that the strong, loving, and faithful example my father had provided for us during his life-time did help us to cope with the unacceptable, personal tragedy of his death as well as to prepare us to carry on in ways that eventually revealed themselves during the ensuing years.

If there *is* something certain in the uncertain field of risk management, it just might be that a firm foundation built on integrity, character, and love may be able to help pull us through even the most devastating of times, no matter how difficult and unsettling the circumstances. These qualities take years of work to develop, but they can provide us with the integrity and strong character, and, yes, even self-esteem that are crucial elements in reacting to improbable and bad events.

Conclusions

I'm one of those people who like to be prepared for anything. I embrace certainty and predictability. I used to believe that I could prepare myself—and my surroundings—so completely and perfectly that everything would go according to plan—always. Working at the asphalt plant taught me that no matter how thoroughly I prepare, I can still be surprised by improbable, unpredictable events. I learned that surprise itself was probable by seeing with my very own eyes that

The strongest things can bend.

The strongest things can break.

REFERENCES

[DEM03]   T. DeMarco and T. Lister, *Waltzing With Bears: Managing Risk on Software Projects* (New York: Dorset House Publishing, 2003).

[OBR04]   R. O'Bryan and D. Phillips, *It Sounded Good When We Started: A Project Manager's Guide to Working With People on Projects* (New York: IEEE Computer Society Press/John Wiley and Sons, 2004).

SEVEN

Practice

It is impossible to manage a project well without observing, planning, and remaining alert. As managers, we perform all of this work as part and parcel of our actual practice—it's what we do. I like the word "practice," as it describes both my actions and the fact that my actions are exercises: I repeat them over and over, trying to master and improve.

I have enjoyed having many years in which to learn and practice, and while I should recognize that other people need time to reach the same level of knowledge, expertise, and understanding that I think I now have reached, I nevertheless still sometimes find myself impatient with people who don't know what I know. I need to constantly remind myself that time is needed for each of us to learn and practice.

I've learned some new piece of information or a refinement of a practice almost every day since I left the asphalt plant, but I learned *how to do many things for the first time* while working at the plant. There, I was taught to do many more tasks that I didn't already know how to do than I was assigned jobs I had already mastered. My days were challenging and full, but the lingering difficulty for me was that the conditions in the workplace weren't quite right for me to absorb everything I was shown when I was shown it. As a result, I often felt inept and lacking, hindered by my inability to catch on quickly. I yearned for more time to practice what I had been shown.

Another reason why I yearned for more time was that I only rarely could work continuously to completion on any given job at the plant, and so a project that required a lot of time to complete had to be performed in chunks of an hour or two every few days.

One very time-consuming project required several years of my effort! I don't recall ever having time enough to work on it for a full day or for several days in a row. Instead, I worked on it an hour here and a few hours there, and, by means of persistent whittling, I eventually finished it. I have seen many overwhelmingly complex and overwhelmingly large and perplexing tasks completed by the same method—one baby-step at a time. Persistent whittling can be effective on tasks as small as one person working one day to eighty people working five long years. The simple one-step-at-a-time method can usually be made to work.

Sometimes, however, simple step-by-step whittling methods don't work. We had one job to perform at the asphalt plant that we knew would require hard work, but we felt confident that we could do it because we saw that there was an obvious method for doing the work. When that method was unsuccessful, our foreman thought for a few moments—and then he invented another method that did work, demonstrating to me the importance of being flexible enough to give up what has been learned—the tried-and-true—in order to substitute something new in its place.

That day troubled me because the need to switch from working according to a learned method to working according to an untried approach went against my very grain. Casting aside what I had learned when it did not work was exceedingly difficult for me. (I *prepare* before working on a task, and the switch to a method I have not prepared for distressed me then, as it does to this day.) However, when the learned method doesn't match reality, I can choose either to adapt—and hope to succeed—or to stick with what does not work—and possibly flounder.

In the end, I should choose to do what works. Doing what works should be simple, but it sometimes has proven to be difficult for me. It is my nature to try to fit in and do what works, rather than stick with what is learned but does not work. Sometimes, I have to force myself to step out of my comfort zone into the unfamiliar.

156

Practice helps me to be able to do something when it is needed, whether or not it is what I have prepared myself to do. At the plant, we needed time to learn how to accomplish work. Day-to-day persistence—practice—when doing difficult tasks greatly increases one's likelihood for success. Most important, however, is time to do what is right.

OPERATING THE FRONT-END LOADER

The "do everything" piece of heavy equipment at the asphalt plant was the front-end loader. The primary function of the front-end loader, of course, was to load sand. It was a big piece of machinery, so big that its bucket could reach some twenty feet high into the air to clear the side of a dump truck.

We used the front-end loader for an incredible number of duties other than just loading dump trucks. In the previous chapter, I described how we rigged a boom and chain onto the front-end loader so that we could use it as a crane, but we also used the front-end loader's bucket as a forklift to transport men and tools up in the air so they could do repair work or paint parts of the plant that were too high up to reach by ladder.

I'd worked at the plant for almost a year when one of the men showed me how to operate the front-end loader. Driving it seemed simple enough because, just like a car, it had a gas pedal for accelerating and a second pedal for braking. There were only two gears—forward and reverse—so that part was much simpler than a car.

The big difference was that the front-end loader also had two levers to operate the bucket lift. Pushing one lever forward raised the bucket from the ground up to about twenty feet; pulling back on the same lever lowered the bucket. The other lever tilted the bucket, allowing the operator to manipulate it to scoop objects up and dump things out. That was all there was to it—I was able to learn the mechanics of operation in less than a minute.

After walking me through the mechanics, the operator said, "Okay, Dwayne, go practice on that mountain of sand at the back of the plant." Then he climbed down from the cab of the front-end loader and walked away. I moved the forward gear, stepped lightly on the accelerator pedal, and easily drove over to the sand pile—so far, so good. But trying to scoop some sand and drop it where I wanted it was a completely different story: For the life of me, I couldn't do it! I am not a complete klutz, but getting the bucket of the front-end loader to move the way I wanted had me completely stymied. The mechanics were simple, but I couldn't operate the machine.

I had been struggling with the beast for about half an hour when the operator came back to regain control of his machine. He explained that although he had a lot of other jobs to do around the plant that afternoon, he might be able to turn it back over to me again for more practice the next day. I was extremely happy to be relieved of the machine, but kept my relief to myself. I only replied, "Sure. Thanks for the time to practice." Then I switched off the motor and jumped down from the cab. As he lumbered up into the control seat, he looked back down at me kindly and remarked, "It just takes some time to get used to it."

That day I learned

Time and practice are often both necessary.

SOME THINGS TAKE TIME

I never mastered the front-end loader. I think I could have become a pretty decent operator if I had had enough time and opportunity to practice, practice, practice, but the managers at Louisiana Paving didn't think it was a good use of what was, in 1970, a $250,000 piece of equipment—plus my hourly wage to let me practice for hours at a time.

I've been able to apply the front-end loader lesson to many situations in the workplace since my days at the plant. One example happened in late 2003 when I moved into a new job, brought in by a senior manager to help instill a culture of systematic planning and engineering in his staff. My new workplace had functioned as an engineering hobby shop to which people came in from the field, bought parts, built the parts into some kind of component, and then took the desired gizmo back with them to the field. This method had worked for years, but the senior manager saw how much the industry had changed during those years, requiring a change in methods.

I came to the new job wanting to learn as much as I could about what people were doing. I spent most of my first weeks talking all day long to people about the projects they had worked on, the products they had built, and how they had used them.

After just a few days, I noticed that I could only absorb just so much information in one day but, as I was being paid for a full eight-hour day, I stuck with my plan to talk to people for all eight hours. After about five or six hours, my head started to spin, and I couldn't listen anymore. This happened day after day until I realized that learning so much new material was similar to learning to operate the front-end loader. The mechanics were simple—listen and write—but the reality of actually practicing what I had learned was something quite different.

I decided that reality should overrule theory. The reality was that there was a limit to how much information I could absorb in one day. Once I hit that limit, I would stop my practice of intake— that is, stop listening—and start to output—writing what I had absorbed on pads of paper as well as entering information into my laptop.

Another piece of wisdom about the importance of *taking time to do a task* as well as the importance of *waiting until the right time* came from a colleague of mine named Mary. Mary grew up on a farm in Michigan where her father both farmed and, as part of farming, trained horses. He taught Mary the importance of postponing serious training until a filly or colt was about two years old. He understood that a horse needed time to grow into its body. Attempts to train a horse before the horse was ready physically would frustrate the trainer and, considerably more devastating, possibly ruin the horse.

Mary took this lesson completely to heart. She practiced taking time to do a task and waiting for the right time when raising her own children and, later, her grandchildren. She understood that children need time to grow into their bodies before they can perform activities that require both practice and developed fine-motor skills. Activities such as hitting a baseball or writing the letters of the alphabet require eye-hand coordination that develops as the body develops and grows.

Most people know that children generally learn to read before they learn to write, but my wife showed me how important it is to provide people (kids are people, too) with time to grow and time to practice when she was helping our sons learn to read. She kept writing lessons on the back-burner because she understood that trying to teach someone to write at the same time he or she is learning to read frustrates everyone, teacher and student alike, and may result in a person's life-long distaste for both writing and reading. I quickly learned that it doesn't do much for a parent either.

MOST PEOPLE TAKE TIME

At this point, if you are a manager reading this chapter, you may be wondering, "What do training horses and teaching small children to read have to do with the troubles I have at work?" I think the two have a strong connection, and that connection is *people*. On the job, we work *with* people and we accomplish work *through* people. We train each other—we mold behavior and alter work processes, and throughout it all, we see proof that most people need time to learn and time to practice.

Another important aspect of knowing and learning is *patience.* When I am patient, I allow another person the time he or she needs to do something. When I am impatient, I show that I have decided how long another person should have to do something.

Impatience seems to me to be the height of arrogance. Who gave me the right to decide how long it will take another person to learn something? Why do I expect other people to learn and do things on my time schedule?

It pains me to admit it, but I am impatient at times—with colleagues, with vendors, with family. On the positive side, I think it is fair to say that I have been far more impatient in the past than I am now. My children, especially during their teenage years, have taught me many valuable lessons about patience that I have since carried to the workplace. I am thankful that they were patient enough to allow me these many years to learn.

Sometimes I favor hiring people to work with me who still have much to learn. Not having learned something—yet—does not signify stupidity. To me, being stupid about something means that

I *cannot* learn. Being ignorant about something means I have not yet learned. I will always take ignorant people over stupid ones.

EVERYONE KNOWS THAT!

I strongly believe the following about people: People don't know everything, what they don't know they can learn, and they require time and practice to learn. You may be thinking, "Everyone knows this about people." To this I reply, "No, they don't."

I graduated from college in 1980 with a bachelor's degree in electrical engineering and entered the workplace where people assumed I knew all the things that every electrical engineer knew. They rattled on about communications using RF technology, (that is, radios and antennas). In college, however, I had written software programs and studied computers—instead of immersing myself in the normal electrical engineering topics of magnetic fields and radio waves.

I didn't understand radios, antennae, or much of anything these people discussed. I tried to tell them what I knew and what I didn't know, but I was intimidated by their experience—and a little afraid that if they discovered how little I knew, I would lose my job.

These electrical engineers assumed that a fresh-out-of-college electrical engineer would know certain things. I was fresh out of college and an electrical engineer, so they decided that they knew what I knew. They were wrong, but from the experience, I learned a bit about not being presumptuous and a bit more about learning.

WORKING WITH LEARNERS

The front-end-loader lesson influenced how I, to this day, hire and fire people—and how I manage work. I call the two models that people learn by *the trade-school model* and *the liberal-arts model*.

The Trade-School Model

Usually, people who have attended a trade school, where they've learned a specific skill, are equipped to perform one job well, but only one job. Hiring practices based on the trade-school model would mean only hiring people who already know how to do the job at hand. Someone who learns how to be an electrician probably has attended a school that teaches nothing but that line of work. The person learns the requisite skills, graduates, and, immediately upon whatever local or state certification is needed, then can work as an electrician. If I need an electrician, I look in the Yellow Pages under the Electrician category, call the telephone number listed for whatever electrician I select, set up an appointment for the work to be done, pay the bill, and then move on.

The trade-school model fits other professions. Computer programmers joined this category in the late 1990s when many of them began working for hire much as an electrician works for hire. Here's how it goes: A company finds itself with a troubled project and needs extra programmers to help finish the work. It contacts an agency that screens programmers for hire, brings in a few contract programmers to work with the permanent staff until the project is completed, and then lets them go.

The trade-school model involves a lot of letting people go (you can think of it as temporary work that ends, or you can think of it as firing). Once a job is finished, the person is fired. I have had electricians come to my home to repair electrical problems. They come in, do the work, and leave after I acknowledge that the job is done, usually after a few hours. I don't use the word "firing" unless they've not done the job to my satisfaction and specification, but one could consider the act of authorizing a worker's departure as a "firing." It's essentially the same thing, but it's a lot easier to do than a real firing involving the worker who has been an employee rather than "for hire" or a contractor.

When I hire by means of the trade-school model, it affects the way I manage work. I do little training, but I do a lot of interviewing, hiring, and firing. In order to run efficient projects, I need to plan ahead, look for employees days and weeks before I need them, and hire them, just in time.

The Liberal-Arts Model

In contrast to the trade-school model is the liberal-arts model. With a liberal-arts education, a person is introduced to many different topics, and then goes on to concentrate in greater depth on one or two major topics. Graduates of liberal-arts colleges are generalists and are not required to learn specialized skills geared to a specific industry. Unless they so elect, they are not trained to write complex computer programs, fix electrical wiring, install plumbing, or do tasks that require detailed technical knowledge and skills. They are trained, however, to think analytically, read for comprehension, write coherently, and form conclusions based on fact, for example.

The advantage that liberal-arts college graduates possibly have over a trade-school graduate is *they have learned how to learn.* They have acquired study skills and can apply them to different situations.

I can use the liberal-arts model to manage work. I do little hiring and firing with this model. Instead, I do continuous training. I need to plan the work, arrange for training, allow learning to occur, and empower people to do what they have learned. I must plan far enough in advance so training and learning will be completed in time for people to do the work. Planning is not easy, and I haven't met many people who do it well. Planning well enough for the liberal-arts model is a big challenge for managers.

As I have noted previously, I have worked for the United States government since 1980. I use the liberal-arts model there because colleges don't teach people how to do the things we do at work. When I first worked for the government, I needed to take what I had learned in college and apply it to learning new tasks at work. The job I do today bears little resemblance to what I did in 1980. I use tools and techniques that did not exist in 1980, let alone in 1990. I had to learn how to use these on the job, after I was hired, so I have gone through many cycles of learning and doing—but at the onset of every cycle, I rethink the best model to follow.

Choosing a Model

The trade-school model and the liberal-arts model each have advantages and disadvantages. Economics plays a part in determining which model is best for a certain job. So do people's personalities. By considering economic issues first, and then moving on to the more decisive factor of personality, I can choose the model that will work best for a given situation. The trade-school model has some economic advantages over the liberal-arts model. For example, there is no training cost as people arrive ready to do their work, and then leave. Temporary employees are less expensive to maintain in the workplace. They don't receive benefits and they don't require as nicely outfitted a work environment as do long-term employees. But, since each business is organized uniquely and tackles projects in different ways, considering economics alone cannot show me which model to choose.

Personality issues also must be considered when choosing between the trade-school model and the liberal-arts model. I must confess that I first saw the trade-school model as cruel and, since I am a product of a liberal-arts approach to a trade-school education, I had a bias against trade-school practices. One reason I thought the trade-school model cruel is that I hate firing anyone. A person earning a living while working for me presumably is supporting himself or herself as well as a family. Once fired, the person is no longer earning a living and supporting loved ones. I can only hope that, despite the cruel firing, the person will find new employment before their life savings expire and they become homeless. Okay, that's possibly a bit dramatic, but you see how my personality and tendency to be pessimistic come into play even when I am considering economics first.

In my acquisition work as a government contractor, I have "fired" a few dozen companies and a few thousand people. Most firings came at the completion of successful projects. The people I "fired" went on to work on other projects and kept earning a living. Nevertheless, each firing hurt me, probably more than it hurt the company or the person who needed to walk.

When I fire someone, I hope to myself: *This is a smart person. She will be able to learn a new skill quickly and keep working.* Or I offer re-training, again hoping to myself: *He will be fine in the next position. He knows how to survive—and he will be back on two feet in no time.*

Sometimes, what I am hoping to myself reflects a selfish attitude. Some people don't want to learn a new skill or work in a new job. Some people love doing one type of thing and would not enjoy doing anything else. Again, personality is a factor as someone with this type of personality flourishes with the trade-school model. For these people, being fired grants them the freedom to find another employer who will pay them to do what they love. In this sense, firing someone after a job is finished is good for everyone.

Using the trade-school model accommodates building relationships with a great variety of people and personalities. In my acquisition position with the United States government, I have worked with dozens of different companies and have learned a great deal of work-related and off-the-wall, unrelated skills from the fine people who worked for them. For example, during my years in government work, I earned a master's degree and then a Ph.D., but in between, I learned to drive big, eighteen-wheel, tractor-trailer rigs. That was fun for me because I like to stay open to change and challenge. My personality is such that I thrive in a workplace in which every new experience helps me accomplish work better.

A manager should know what his or her staff members' or coworkers' preferences are. The best way I know to access this information is to ask people directly. Sometimes I can accommodate a person's preference, but not always. I try to tell people what model we will use in the workplace before we make any other arrangements. That affords both parties the chance to sever the relationship before either invests resources in it.

Thoughts on the Front–End Loader

I wish I had had more time to practice operating the front-end loader. Although I am pretty sure I could have become a good operator, this may be a wishful remembrance. Perhaps the front-end-loader operator—as the operator of record—realized then and there that he would have had a difficult time explaining to his management why he let some college kid fool around with a pricey and extremely valuable piece of machinery.

I did learn how to drive and operate dump trucks at the plant. While not as simple as driving a car, operating a dump truck did not require as much coordination and practice as the front-end loader. Maybe I had more aptitude for it, or maybe it took less time and practice to learn, but I got pretty good at operating dump trucks by the time I left the plant.

Since those days, I have learned how to do other things that take a long time and a lot of practice to master. I needed about five years to learn how to write a book, and then I needed another five years to learn how to write a second book. No one was paying me to do this learning, which leads me to surmise that book publishers use the trade-school model when "hiring" authors. After all these years, I think I may have come full circle and am ready to leave the world of the liberal-arts model and enter the trade-school model world of skilled (but often unemployed) workers.

PAINTING BLACK AND YELLOW STRIPES

The asphalt plant was three stories tall. Each story had a walkway around it and stairs leading to the next section. The walkways and stairs had safety rails made of angled iron—flat pieces of metal bent to a 90-degree angle to make an L. Each walkway had two safety rails, one about waist height and the other about knee height.

The safety rails were battleship gray, like the rest of the plant, and needed black and yellow stripes painted on them to make them stand out from the gray walkways and stairs. My supervisor at the time was my dad, and he asked me paint these black and yellow stripes in my spare time. I never quite understood why black and yellow stripes made the safety rails safer, but safety was the reason my dad gave me when he told me to paint the stripes.

In retrospect, maybe the safety rails really didn't need painting; maybe my father had me do this job to keep me busy while the plant was paying me an hourly wage. At any rate, equipped with one small brush, many cans of black paint and yellow paint, and one "tool"—wood cut from a two-by-four—I did the job and painted the stripes. The "tool" was a piece of wood, maybe six inches long with 45-degree-angle cuts on each end. I used the wood as a pattern, holding it tight against the flat, gray safety rail so that I could mark the rail with a pencil to show the angled lines. After I marked a twenty-foot section of rail, I would paint every other marked part with yellow paint. Then I walked back to where I had started the section, and then I painted the alternating sections with black paint.

Painting the outer sections of angled iron wasn't too difficult, but painting the undersides of rail was pure torture. I had to bend over the rails and reach back up underneath to mark the lines with pencil and then paint them. To prepare and paint the lower rail, I had to be on my knees and bend over like a contortionist to reach the underside. I had to assume this cramped position high above the ground three times for every section.

Painting the black stripes and yellow stripes was a slow and nasty job. I needed a couple of hours to paint about three feet of railing. Since the rails wrapped around two levels of the asphalt plant as well as the stairs that led from the ground up through the two levels, it took me most of two years to paint it all.

When I finally finished painting the stripes and thought about all the time required and about how I completed the task six inches at a time, I realized that I'd learned an important lesson to carry with me through life:

A little work, repeated, can accomplish much.

ONE STEP AT A TIME

I was proud of myself after I finished painting all those black and yellow stripes. I felt satisfaction, having taken one step at a time until I completed what I have since come to see as a long and arduous journey. Finishing jobs still is important to me, but I don't believe I've ever had to complete a job as seemingly endless as that one at the plant.

I forgot about accomplishing big jobs by means of many small steps soon after I left the plant, but one day, the experience came back to me. Working in a foreign country at a primitive workplace far from home, I found myself in a horrendously cluttered and disorganized storage room looking for materials and supplies my project had shipped to this isolated location. Clearly, someone had "unloaded" the shipment by throwing everything willy-nilly into the storage room. There were plenty of sturdy shelves lining the walls, but all of the materials, parts, and supplies had been dumped out of their boxes and cartons into piles all over the floor. Fighting an overwhelming urge to abandon my search and go to lunch a couple of hours early, I decided that the only way I could find the materials I needed was to sort through the piles and put items on shelves, even if it took me several days.

I picked up an item from the floor, examined it for its part number, and placed it on a low shelf to correspond with its low part number. I picked up the next item from the floor, examined it, and placed it on another shelf, ordered by part number. I kept on picking and shelving, organizing supplies and materials and parts, one by one, according to function or color or whatever seemed to fit. I continued this slow, boring, backbreaking process until eventually there were no more items on the floor. I had placed everything neatly on shelves, transforming the frightful, crowded storage room into a seemingly spacious and welcoming space. I had organized items while I worked—and now I could find anything I wanted quickly and easily.

I gathered up the materials I had come for and then looked at my watch to see the time. I could not believe my eyes when I discovered that this long and boring process of cleaning and organizing the storage room had consumed just a little more than two hours. That had to be wrong. All this work, this seemingly never-ending task, had to have consumed days, not just a few hours.

As I walked from the storage room to catch the end of lunch, I marveled at how all I had done was pick up one item at a time and place it on a shelf. Moving one object at a time was like painting one stripe at a time on the asphalt plant's safety rails—it took time and patience, but it got the job done. I had done a similar task before—putting empty boxes to use for storage in my cluttered office—but I felt satisfied to have accomplished it.

The lessons of painting stripes and moving one object at a time have stayed with me. During the twenty years following my storage-room epiphany, I worked at several other isolated facilities. Each seemed to have its own version of the disorganized storage room, with everything discarded on the floor despite plenty of empty shelves. On several occasions, I found myself in the company of another person who would gasp in horror at the mess. Telling my companion not to worry, I'd reassuringly explain, "All we have to do is pick up one item at a time and place it on a shelf. We'll be done in just a few hours." No one ever believed me until we had organized the storage room—in an hour or two.

Thoughts on One Step at a Time

I have written five books and close to one hundred papers prior to writing this book. I wrote each piece one word at a time. No, on closer reflection, I see that I wrote each piece one keystroke at a time.

One keystroke on a keyboard doesn't require much work, but the trick to writing a book or an essay is selecting the proper key to hit for each keystroke and then repeating that little keystroke action for just the right number of strikes. The lesson is not subtle—doing things takes time and practice, but it also takes selection.

IGNORING THE STRIPES

The lessons gleaned while painting stripes and picking objects one item at a time also apply to real jobs that matter to the health and welfare of government agencies and private companies, both large and small. I have known managers over the years who failed to appreciate how satisfying it is to complete jobs by taking one step at a time, all the while paying attention to the stripes.

One of the most painful experiences I know of involved some of my coworkers on the $40 million project Roy O'Bryan and I describe in *It Sounded Good When We Started* (*see* [OBR04] *and* [PHI04]). Recap the scene: The contractor was building a system for the government and was behind schedule and eager to do something *quickly* to recover lost time. It reached the point at which it was ready to embark on a period of "bottom-up" building and testing. It had built all the small parts and tested each individually to determine that the small parts all worked; then it combined them into medium-sized parts and tested those medium-sized parts to verify that what it had built would continue to work; and finally, it was ready to combine the medium-sized parts into one complete system and test it.

The bottom-up approach is much like painting black and yellow stripes. It is a slow process, but one that eventually leads to a complete, working system. The contractor, however, wanted to skip all the intermediate build-and-test steps and instead urged the government to allow it to use the "big bang" approach, building the entire system and then testing it all at once. There was enormous risk in this approach—if the system worked, the contractor would have saved a lot of time. If the system didn't work, the problem (or, more likely, many problems) could be in any one or several of the little or mid-sized parts of the system. Because none of the little, mid-sized, or complete system parts would have been individually tested when using this approach, there would be no sure way to quickly locate a problem.

The government decided that the contractor knew what it was doing, and allowed it to skip all the little, slow, boring, build-and-test steps, combining everything into one big build and test. The result was not surprising: The system didn't work. There were hundreds of failed steps in testing, and because each failure had several possible causes, no one knew which causes were responsible for which failure.

The project plan had called for a six-week systems test. Because the contractor, with the government's approval, had skipped all the little build-and-test steps, it needed nine months to complete the test. In its haste to make up schedule, the contractor fell further behind. In retrospect, the contractor was exceedingly foolish to attempt the big-bang approach, and the government was equally foolish to approve it.

Foolish shortcuts bring to mind comparisons between my workplace and the fast-food society in which Americans live. When I walk into fast-food restaurants and see eighteen-year-old kids preparing meals literally in seconds, I wonder why the adults where I work take so long to do anything? One of the probable reasons is that what adults attempt to accomplish at work is generally more complex than making hamburgers.

It is easy, however, to gather false impressions from the fast-food industry. For example, when I order my burger and receive it in seconds, I don't see everything that makes this happen. The vast majority of the work occurs before the teenage worker or I walk into the fast-food facility. Ranchers raise cattle; farmers raise wheat and vegetables; and food manufacturers prepare ketchup, mustard, and myriad other condiments. Most of the ingredients are shipped with intricate timing by rail and truck so that they arrive at the designated location on the right day. Little of this work is accomplished by eighteen-year-olds; still less is accomplished without patient management; surely none of it is accomplished in seconds.

ADULT WORK

I work with adults. Most readers of this book also work with adults to perform what we consider to be adult work, which requires vision, focus, patience, and, sometimes, swallowing one's pride. My work—even my work painting stripes and organizing storage rooms—usually begins with a *vision.* I didn't appreciate it at the time, but when my father gave me the funny-shaped block of wood, a pencil, a paintbrush, and a couple of cans of paint so many years ago, he also gave me a vision of what completion of the job would mean. Even before I'd drawn the first line, he helped me to see that those ugly, gray, safety rails could be transformed by black and yellow safety stripes.

I'm currently working on a five-year, $90 million project, and I struggle to correlate what I am doing today with the end of the project. A vision of what our work will bring in five years helps me to see the importance of today's one-step-at-a-time.

While my vision of the end of a project helps me keep going in the right direction, my *focus* on little, daily steps can help me to advance without stumbling. If, for example, I need to convince a budget staff to commit a small portion of funds to a sub-project that is under my current five-year project, I may need to keep the vision of the five-year project's culmination in my mind in order to write a three-line memo to the budget staff to convince it of the sub-project's merit in light of the project itself. Focusing on keeping my five-year project moving forward helps me to concentrate on each word in the memo so as to convey the required information in a brief and concise manner.

Vision also requires *patience.* While writing that little three-line memo, I wanted to scream at people. They should have understood the importance of the funding without my having to focus so hard. One word from me should have been sufficient for instant action. Instead, I had to think and craft the memo slowly and surely.

Adult work performed in accord with the lesson of the black and yellow stripes sometimes requires swallowing some pride.

When I left graduate school, I had to work on my dissertation at home in the evenings and on weekends. I remember that when I started working on the dissertation, I told myself that I didn't have time to make and correct mistakes in the computer programs I would write. It sounds silly to recall this, but I told myself over and over again, "No mistakes, no mistakes."

Of course I made mistakes—many mistakes—and spent lots of time correcting them. That is the nature of work; we all make mistakes. I had to swallow some pride before I would admit this to myself. Every time I made a programming mistake, I first spent time chastising myself for the error; then I spent time correcting the error. All that time I spent chastising was wasted, as it didn't prevent me from making mistakes in the future. Denying that mistakes will be made only wastes time and effort. I finally learned that the most efficient way to work was to swallow my pride, accept that I make mistakes, and work in a manner that lessens the cost of mistakes.

PAINTING BEGINS WITH A "P"

The lesson I learned from painting black stripes and yellow stripes has affected the way I manage adult work. One way I organize my actions as a manager is with a series of four "P" words: *plan, persevere, perform,* and *pat* (on the back).

Plan

The first step I take in managing adult work is to *plan* the work. I had a plan when I started painting the black and yellow stripes. (Well, maybe I didn't, but my father surely did.) My father arranged my schedule so that I could do the work in small, manageable chunks. I probably never painted stripes for more than two hours at a time. The fact that I only had a limited amount of time each time I painted and the fact that I had only one "tool" in addition to supplies of a brush, paint, and a pencil kept me from making big mistakes that would require big rework to correct.

Had I remembered my painting lesson when the contractor requested approval to use the big-bang approach and proposed skipping bottom-up build-and-test, I believe I would have opposed its plan. The contractor did have a plan, but its plan didn't break the work into small, logical, and manageable chunks. It attempted one large piece of work that was risky and difficult to manage, and it's no wonder it failed, and failed big.

Persevere

After my plan is ready, my next step is to do the work until it's done—and that means I must *persevere.* Plans that employ small steps sometimes lead to repetitive work. I have found a strong correlation between work that is repetitive and work that is successful. Repeating a task builds skill, and skill usually leads to success. Repetitive work is often boring, however, and doing work that is boring requires perseverance. I believe I acquired my ability to persevere during the two years I labored intermittently at the plant painting stripes.

Perseverance, like most things, can be taken too far. I recommend that people make plans and stay with them. I also recommend against becoming slaves to our plans. We make plans early in a project at a time when we know the least about the work. As we proceed, we learn about the project and what we are really trying to accomplish. This knowledge enables us to create a much better plan. I often re-plan a project while in the middle of it. The result is usually much better than staying with the original plan from start to finish.

Perform

My next step is to *perform* the actual work, a step that is difficult for me because I love to sit back and create the master plan. Once the plan is in motion and people are working, I am ready to move on to another big problem that requires a plan.

Performing work differs from planning work. Planning involves big concepts and a vision of a distant future. Performing work is dipping the brush into the paint can and carefully applying paint inside the pencil marks. Performing work is pressing a key on the keyboard for the twenty-thousandth letter to finish chapters of a book. Performing work means going to the workplace each day to accomplish small chunks of work that constitute a tiny piece of the big vision. Performing work is difficult because it takes so much discipline, but many people can perform work well when given a good plan and lots of encouragement (regarding the latter, see the next section).

I have a personal conflict with planning and performing work. I love to move on to the next big thing, but I perform the tedious work leading to completed projects more diligently than do most people. The Myers-Briggs Type Indicator seems to explain this situation best. I am an ISTJ in my preferences. For people who haven't studied Myers-Briggs, being an ISTJ means that I am a typical, boring engineer (*see* [KEI84]; [MYE80], *and* [WEI97], *for further discussion*).

My preference is to work through problems and challenges until I resolve them. That I have chosen to write books and that I actually complete them for publication is an example of the kind of "problem" I work through and resolve. Many people come up with ideas for books and submit proposals to publishers, and publishers accept many of the proposals for publication, but a surprisingly sizable number of those would-be authors don't finish their manuscripts and, therefore, never submit them for publication. As an ISTJ, I carry the ball, no matter how tedious, from beginning to end.

Given the variety in preferences and personalities, I recommend taking great care in recruiting staff for projects. Adult work requires some people who can conceive big ideas and plan projects, as well as some people who can work through each little step in the plan. A group with one type of person but not the other usually leads to failed projects.

A Pat on the Back

I like to encourage people with a figurative *pat on the back* as often as I can. I encourage people, both figuratively and literally, before they start a task. I continue to encourage them throughout the work; and I express appreciation for their efforts at the end, regardless of the outcome. Sometimes, people object when I pat other people on the back. A not-uncommon reaction is, "You want to reward whom? For doing what? That little accomplishment isn't worthy of reward. They're just doing their job."

That the accomplishment is little is a side effect of planning work in small chunks. People only accomplish a small chunk of work at a time. Patting someone on the back after he or she has completed a small bit of work is a good thing to do. I call such people "positive workers" because they move the work one step at a time in the right direction. If we repeat that progress many times over a period of time, we will accomplish an impressive amount of work.

I also like to pat people on the back who have performed a task well—no matter how small the task—because not all work that gets done gets done well. To the best of my knowledge, no one has passed a law that says people have to show up every day and do "good work." I have seen people come to work day after day and accomplish little or nothing. I think of these people as "zero workers" because they don't accomplish anything positive, but there are workers who are even worse than "zero workers."

Such people come to work day after day and set back the work of others. I think of these people as "negative workers" because they consume the time and resources of other people, and they keep them from their work. It would seem reasonable to believe that "negative workers" are quickly fired, but when I talk to managers at a variety of companies and industries throughout the World, they confirm that just the opposite is true. Proving that someone is a negative influence is more difficult than it would appear.

Given the possibility of "zero workers" and "negative workers," I am happy when I work with "positive workers." I try my best to tell them how much I appreciate what they do.

Thoughts on Painting Black and Yellow Stripes

I usually visit my mother in Louisiana two or three times a year and, during these visits, I occasionally drive on Highway 51, past the asphalt plant. From the highway, I can see the black stripes and yellow stripes on the safety rails, and every time I see them, I am amazed at what I accomplished. There are few jobs I have done in my life that have had such long-lasting results as those stripes I painted back in the late 1970s. It is gratifying to see them, after all these years.

While painting all those stripes, I had to stay with "the plan," even on days when I didn't feel like doing so. That required perseverance. Maybe perseverance was what my father was hoping to instill in me. Whether that was his plan, I'll never be able to know, but every time I see the stripes, I send up to my father another appreciative pat on the back. Thanks again, Dad.

WET ROCKS AND HOT DAYS

On at least one occasion during my summers working at the asphalt plant, I had to unload tons of rocks from railroad cars—a completely memorable experience, to say the least. Our asphalt mixture required a special type of rock, which came into the plant in railroad cars along a siding that connected with nearby railroad tracks.

The theory of how we were to go about unloading the rocks was simple: We would slide open a trapdoor in the floor of the railroad car and the rocks would shoot out into a cargo container positioned below the track. Because all four of the inside walls of the railroad cars slanted to form a giant chute, once a car's door was opened, gravity would force the rocks to the bottom of the car and out the opening.

Reality quickly challenged this theory. The summer day I was assigned to work as one of three laborers tackling the task, open-top railroad cars rolled into position carrying rain-soaked rocks. We soon discovered that wet rocks don't slide out an open door. Instead, they stick to one another and to the sides of the railroad car. To slide the rocks out, I had to climb up to the top of each railroad car, balance myself precariously on its edge so I would not fall, and jab repeatedly at the rocks with a heavy steel rod.

I did this on a cloudless and unbearably hot and humid 95° F day, made all the more unbearable because the slanted sides of the cars formed reflectors. The glare from the sun bounced back up at me, and the heat of the day turned the water in the rocks into steam for me to soak up as I banged away with that heavy steel rod.

We worked with the steaming rocks for several hours straight and, by the time we called it quits, I was thoroughly soaked from head to toe. That experience taught me the hard way that a task that is supposed to be easy—open a door and watch rocks slide out—can be surprisingly difficult. Moreover, I learned that

Believing that theory equals reality can bring surprisingly unpleasant, bad results.

This Is *Not* What They Told Me!

Don't get the impression that I think all theory useless. Theory, in spite of sporadic conflict with reality, can be useful to managers. The best theory evolves out of practice. At some point, someone observes specific things happening that support a conclusion. That someone then forms a general description or idea, which becomes theory.

Some theories prove to be true the vast majority of the time. Gravity is one such case. I depend on it every day and have yet to find a case in which the theory of gravity disagrees with reality. Therefore, when I am about to drop a heavy object, I make sure first that my feet are not below it.

There are some management theories that usually conform to reality. For example, there is no free lunch, people do make mistakes, people do disappoint the ones they love, and being a relative of the boss doesn't make *you* right.

I have experienced many occasions in my professional life in which theory and reality did not match. The surprise caused by some of these mismatches was unpleasant. One notable occasion was in the mid-1980s after I had finished graduate school and returned to work. The theory of my job was simple—I was to finish building a system for installation in a foreign country. I was to move my family to that foreign country, install the system, and live with it for two years. The country in question wasn't going to be a nice place to live, and so, in light of the living hardship and the technical expertise required, I was to be promoted the day I arrived on the job.

The reality was neither simple nor pleasant. On the first day I reported for work, I discovered that my new managers had no idea why I thought I was to have been promoted—and no amount of conversation could convince them otherwise. I immersed myself in the job of finishing the system in anticipation of installing it overseas. Then, another blow from reality: Major political problems meant that the system would not be taken overseas for installation and operation. Instead, I was to close out the system's contracts, dismantle the system, and salvage it for parts. In short, no promotion, no overseas assignment, no nothing.

I was crushed by these events. My wife and I had bought a house in an out-of-the-way community that was perfectly situated for the job I had to tackle, but the location was certain to be terrible now that I was going to have to change jobs. I was stuck with no apparent way out until bad turned miraculously to good when, through the grapevine, I learned of an opening at another foreign post. It was pure dumb luck that the person doing the hiring just happened to live in the same out-of-the-way community where my family and I were now stuck. I visited with him one morning and we chatted for a few hours, first about country living, farming, and restoring old cars, and then about the assignment.

That morning's affable conversation was key to my being asked to fill the open position, and so we sold the house we'd just moved into, packed up our belongings, and moved again, this time with much happier results. The new assignment was professionally gratifying, and my family and I grew to love our new country and home. In fact, we were sorry to leave it after enjoying two happy years there. I will always be glad that things turned out as they did.

Theory and reality again collided when I was back working for the United States government, this time as a kind of government point man with whom people on a dozen different projects could consult. The collision came about when a manager on one of the projects left for another job and my managers asked me to step in to manage the project. My managers told me that the contractor already had passed the difficult milestones in the project, and that it would be smooth sailing to the end. All I would have to do—other than attend a few meetings—was watch the project coast to a successful end.

When I heard that glowing job description, I was a lot older and wiser than I had been that day at the asphalt plant as I set off with my fellow laborers to perform the theoretically easy task of unloading rocks from railroad cars, and so I viewed the job description with considerable skepticism. I well understood that stepping in at the eleventh hour to manage a project to its successful end would be a healthy career move, but I knew just as well that if the project ultimately failed, it possibly would mean an end to my dreams of an early promotion. I spoke with several managers to learn what they thought was this project's likelihood of success, and then I took the job, hoping it would proceed smoothly but prepared for the surprises that reality might bring.

From the get-go, the reality was that this project was a nightmare, exceeding both its budget and its completion schedule by more than 50 percent. The team and I suffered through months of anguish and disappointment. Believe me, it was so horrendous that I even had days when I would hide in a stall in the men's restroom because that was the only place I could go where people would not bring me more bad news about the project.

Eventually, this project yielded some good news. Our users were willing to extend the delivery schedule. They also provided additional money when the budget for the project was exceeded. The contractor used the extra resources wisely and built a good product, which the users are happy with—so happy, in fact, that the contractor has not been able to update individual product units as planned. The units are scattered in the field, and the users won't bring them back long enough for updating.

There were several happy endings to this project. I was promoted for the work I did—as was the contractor's final project manager. In addition, Roy O'Bryan and I centered *It Sounded Good When We Started* on this project.

BEING PREPARED

When I am caught unprepared, I usually perform poorly. To manage effectively, I should be prepared for whatever departure from theory reality throws my way, but experience shows that I cannot be prepared for everything.

My solution is to be prepared for reality to stray from theory. I try to imagine worst-case scenarios, and then I take measures to be prepared for such events should they occur. For example, I've identified one small-scale but nevertheless embarrassing scenario that might occur during lunchtime training sessions that I schedule from time to time for my staff and coworkers. Before these sessions, I work in my own office to prepare slides on my PC that I subsequently will be able to show atttendees while we eat, and I reserve a nearby meeting room in which to hold the training sessions. The theory is that I should be able to walk into the specific meeting room I've reserved, log onto the demo computer that is connected to our office LAN, and display my presentation slides. The worst-case I must be prepared for is that sometimes reality doesn't match theory.

To save myself the embarrassment and frustration of arriving alongside my staff and coworkers, only to find that the meeting-room computer doesn't work, I go to the room a few hours before lunchtime and test the computer. If it doesn't work, I have time either to ask a LAN administrator to correct the problem or to switch the session to a different meeting room. If I know I won't have time to visit the designated room in advance, I prepare for the chance that the computer won't work by bringing a dozen or so sets of paper copies of my slides. Using the paper copies as handouts and the white board that is present in each meeting room, I can give the session I've prepared.

The steps I've described in the preceding paragraphs are neither surprising nor ingenious; they are just practical. There is one additional practical way I handle situations in which the theory I've based my preparation on differs from reality. This additional way does require me to swallow my pride in front of my audience because, on such an occasion, I must admit, "I am sorry, but I am not prepared for what seems to be happening here." Depending on the circumstances, my next sentence could be, "Here's what I think we can do. . . ." or "What do you think we should do?" Depending again on the situation, I might add, "I feel embarrassed by not being prepared. I'd really appreciate hearing your ideas on what we each can learn from this."

I wasn't prepared to be unprepared earlier in my career, and those around me suffered as a result. For example, I didn't know what to say when my promised promotion and overseas assignment disappeared. I could have told senior managers, "This outcome is far from what I anticipated. I am not prepared for this, personally or professionally. What can we do to bring reality back a little closer to what we planned?"

Instead of saying these things and enlisting the managers' help, I blamed the managers. I said, "You guys told me one thing and now you are telling me something else. You are at fault. You owe me." That didn't do any good whatsoever.

When unprepared for a situation, I try to formulate statements beginning with "I." These *I* statements are about me and tell what I am experiencing. Statements beginning with "you" usually put the other person on the defensive because they sound like I am blaming the other person. People whom I seem to be blaming usually don't side with me and certainly don't willingly help me to succeed. In such situations, everyone suffers, the work we perform is harmed, and I fail as a manager.

BELIEVE REALITY

Given that theory and reality often conflict, I must decide what to do to succeed as a manager. First, I try to recognize that the theory may not fit the situation, and then I focus on how best to believe reality. Theories are just theories; someone created them by thinking about how things should be.

I have to be careful when observing what seems to be real. I also must be careful that what I see can be believed. Sometimes, what I see may be a mistaken measurement. For example, I wear a mechanical watch that contains springs and gears. Sometimes, it runs fast; often, it runs slow. If my watch indicates that I am fifteen minutes behind schedule and therefore will be late to a meeting, I check another timepiece—my cellular phone, for example—before I run down the hall. I check reality twice to ensure what is what before acting on it.

Changing direction when faced with reality can be difficult to do: For me to change direction, I first must admit that the theory I have based my plan on is wrong—and therefore, that my plan most probably is wrong. Carrying this thought process a step further, I must admit that I, too, am wrong. Sometimes, I only admit this to myself. (Admitting that the plan is wrong may be impossible for those of us who struggle with the theory that everything we do must be perfect. Reality disagrees with the perfection theory. The imperfection theory, however, has applied to every person I have ever met.)

If I can admit to myself that my theory is at odds with reality, I should then be able to admit it to others. This, too, can be difficult, especially in organizations that punish people who make mistakes. Some people believe that lying hides the truth, but reality disagrees with that theory, too.

If you manage managers, I encourage you to allow them and the people they manage to admit it when reality proves contrary to their theories. At the asphalt plant back all those years ago, we traversed a set of complex activities in short order as we struggled to unload those wet rocks. Operating under the theory that all we had to do was open the door at the bottom of the railroad car to let the rocks slide out, we could have denied reality and stood by waiting for the rocks to move. We might still be standing there now, some thirty years later. Instead, we told our managers about what was happening—the reality. None of the managers told us that we were stupid or lazy for daring to disagree with theory. They believed the reality and had us change direction, sending me up to the top of each car's high side to bang at the wet rocks with a heavy steel rod.

I work with reality until something changes my plan and gives me a new plan—a new theory. Nothing says that the new theory will be perfect either. The first theory wasn't perfect, so it is possible that this one may also be flawed

Thoughts on Wet Rocks and Hot Days

I have attempted some challenging tasks since leaving the asphalt plant, but few, if any, have been quite like the challenge of coaxing wet rocks to slide out of those railroad cars. The difficulty of the task was completely unexpected, coming as it did on my first day back at the plant after my summer classes had ended. When I showed up for work that morning, I had no inkling that I would be doing anything out of the ordinary. My theory was that this day would be just like every other day, but reality soon proved that theory wrong.

What I recall most vividly about that day was how incredibly hot and steamy it was. I have experienced plenty of heat and humidity, having lived, as I did, in Louisiana for almost thirty years. I've also lived in such hot and steamy parts of the world as

Hong Kong; Karachi, Pakistan; and Lagos, Nigeria. In none of those places, however, did I ever experience a day that even came close to matching the heat and humidity I suffered that day while perched on top of the railroad cars.

From just that one day laboring between the Sun and hot, wet rocks, I know that reality sometimes does fly in the face of theory. I am glad I know that. Knowing that I need to believe in what I have experienced *rather than believing in theory* has served me well in the intervening years.

THE ROAD CREW'S LUNCH BREAK

As I've reported previously, I was assigned to a road crew the very first day I worked for Louisiana Paving. The crew was assigned to overlay a twenty-mile stretch of highway, but before we could overlay, we had to construct and set up Road Work Ahead signs along the route.

We spent the entire first day erecting signs at pre-set intervals along the route. As soon as we arrived at a sign location, we would hop off the trucks, dig holes to put the posts in, and fill the holes around the posts so that the signs stayed upright, fixed in place. We would then hop back onto one of the trucks, drive five or so minutes to the next location, and repeat the process.

My dad had suggested that I bring my lunch to work, and so I had packed my lunch box with two ham-and-cheese sandwiches, a thermos, and some corn chips. I brought lunch to the job site ready for the moment the foreman would call a break. As this was my first day working at Louisiana Paving, I really didn't want to do anything wrong, so I waited for the foreman to declare a break. I waited through the mid-morning, through mid-day, and all through the afternoon, but the foreman never called lunch.

I kept myself busy digging signpost holes, and somehow made it through the day without eating. At the end of the day, when the road crew dropped me at the side of the road where my father would pick me up on his way home from the plant, I was so hungry that I practically inhaled the contents of my lunch box. There wasn't a crumb left when my father slowed his car to a stop and I climbed into the passenger's seat. Twenty minutes later, we reached home where I proceeded to gobble down the dinner my mother had waiting for us.

As we ate, my mother asked how my day had been. Between swallows, I told her about the work I had done, suddenly realizing that I had worked a lot that day. I mentioned that as I usually was the first to grab the post-hole digger at each stop, I hadn't really noticed what the rest of the crew was doing while I dug. Then I told my mother that the day was so busy that we never had a lunch break. My father stopped chewing mid-bite and explained to me that Louisiana Paving road crews didn't ever stop work for an official lunch break. "The men eat lunch when they have a chance, Dwayne." He took another small bite of food, swallowed, and then continued, "If there are no good chances to eat, you just stop working and eat when you feel like it. As long as you don't take a long time to eat, no one will mind."

I learned a big lesson that first day at work:

Sometimes no one will tell you when to do something good for yourself.

IT WAS MY TURN

During the early 1990s when I worked at the signal-processing lab, I suffered through many painful assignments, yet a few jobs I did there were pleasant. One of my more enjoyable jobs was managing software development and maintenance work. The dozen programmers working under my direction were smart, hardworking people who taught me a great deal and had a positive influence on how I would spend the ensuing years of my professional life.

During the difficult times, I read a good number of books on the topic of managing technical work. Once assigned the job of managing software development and maintenance, I wanted to try out some techniques from the books. I knew there were more good things I could do as a manager, and figured that some of my book-learning just might help me do them. No one was telling me to do something good, but my memories of the lunch-break lesson reinforced my wish to "do something good" for myself and for those working under my direction.

I decided to try out some of what I had read. First, I drafted a project plan for the big project assigned to me. This began as a personal exercise to see whether I could write a plan like the ones I had studied in the books. I showed the plan to one person at a time, eventually getting up enough nerve to show it to the lab's director, who was suitably impressed when he saw it.

That approval spurred me on to further use. When the project grew unexpectedly, I was able to use the plan to introduce new people to the project. The plan enabled each new person to read about the project for an hour or so, and then start contributing, virtually right away. It was exhilarating to realize that a management technique I had learned from the books had real merit on the job.

Another good thing I did without being told was to form a special interest group on software. I called it SIGSOFT, after a group I had read about in a journal published by the Association for Computing Machinery. Our special interest group met once each month for two or so hours to discuss the different projects we were working on. People talked about a problem they were facing, and someone usually suggested a good solution to the problem, demonstrating to all of us that the SIGSOFT meetings worked. I was surprised to see how many people came to these meetings voluntarily.

I was on a high. Here I was, a new manager, introducing ideas that no one told me to use, and they were working! I was emboldened to keep experimenting, and soon used another idea I had read about, this time to keep our programmers from being interrupted so many times each day. Before I put what I had read into practice, our programmers were lucky to be able to work half an hour without interruption. The idea was so simple that I almost felt foolish, but I went ahead and made up big signs on poster board that advised, "Do not disturb before 10 A.M. or after 3 P.M."

I taped these posters to the doors and walls of our programmers' offices and cubicles. These signs let everyone know that our programmers would attend meetings and carry on ad-hoc discussions during the middle of the day, but that they needed to work *undisturbed* at other times. Of course, some people ignored the signs or took them as a challenge to show they could disrupt work as they pleased—there's one in every crowd!—but most people abided by the restriction and let their colleagues work.

Another oddity about the lab was that we didn't know how much money each different type of work was costing us because the programmers were all contractors. The government paid their companies directly, usually monthly or quarterly but sometimes only once a year. The programmers showed up at the lab for work each day that they were under contract, and they did whatever came their way. The users and analysts frequently asked the programmers to perform small tasks they could have done themselves, primarily because they held the view that work handed over to a programmer cost nothing. The attitude was, "If these programmers don't do something for me, they'll do something for someone else. So, they might as well do something for me."

To find out what the real cost of the programmers' work was, I requested a copy of the contract for each programmer in order to prepare a record showing how much money we paid the parent companies for each person's hours. Next, I typed the salary rates into a spreadsheet, taking care to keep information about specific individuals completely confidential. Then I asked each programmer to fill in a weekly time-card that reported how many hours were spent each week on each job assignment.

When a person completed work on one job or project, I entered the total hours into my spreadsheet and calculated the cost per job or project. Whenever I had the total cost for a completed job or project, I reported the total to lab management, usually at weekly meetings. After a few months of reports, everyone at the lab began to see that we were paying real money for the work the contractors were performing. We all understood that the software work was decidedly not free.

Once the managers realized just how much the programmers cost, they began to think more carefully about the jobs the programmers performed. Some jobs were worth the money spent, while others were not. Now, the managers analyzed each software job and vetoed some of the work requested, instead having the programmers do jobs that they could see justified the cost. The result was that the programmers spent their time doing work that people really wanted instead of work that happened to pop into someone's head. Most of the users were happy and so were the programmers.

Some users, however, were not happy with this arrangement. They objected to having lab managers seem to question their judgment when they requested assistance from the programmers. These analysts and users were insulted by the new practice and were infuriated whenever the lab managers disapproved of their requests.

The group of unhappy users taught me another lesson: "Something good" means "something good *to some people.*" Unanimous acceptance is rare, and there will probably be someone who does not like what someone else decides to do.

Nowadays, before embarking on doing something good without having been invited to do it, I find out who is likely to agree that it will be good and who is likely to disagree. I then mentally weigh how much I need to value the opinion of the different groups of people. Once I know that, I am in a better position to decide whether I want to try the idea. Regardless of my decision, I have come to terms with the fact that even though some people will like what I do, there will be others who won't.

Not everything I tried was a success. Some techniques failed miserably, while other ideas were so resented that they didn't last a day. In the end, however, I think that doing good things without anyone telling me to do them is wise. One small bit of proof that this is true came after I left the lab. A person who had been a harsh critic of mine took charge of my beloved SIGSOFT—the special interest group on software. He, too, saw the value in that little idea, and asked the lab managers to allow him to manage that effort. To paraphrase a cliché, I was flattered by his imitation.

BILLBOARDS

I spent a good part of my childhood riding in the family car. One set of my grandparents lived in Southern California while the other set lived in Louisiana, and we made the long drive back and forth several dozen times. Whenever we crossed Arizona on Interstate 10, we would watch for signs hyping one or another of the roadside attractions that used to dot the American landscape. The particular signs that had us obsessed promised that we would soon come upon "The Thing." For hours as we approached this place from either direction, we watched for the giant, yellow billboards that gave clues about The Thing. We competed to be the first to read each billboard as we tried to guess what exotic object The Thing might be.

When one year we finally convinced our parents to stop so that we could see The Thing with our very own eyes, we were disappointed to learn that it was only a petrified body that had been buried in the nearby desert many centuries earlier. I was, I guess, too young to be impressed by the sight of a body preserved for centuries in the dry desert climate and I let my disappointment in The Thing be known. Other odds and ends on exhibit, such as what was claimed to have been Hitler's Rolls Royce, were more to my liking.

Life as I live it today doesn't have billboards announcing what is ahead. There are no giant, yellow signs that pop out of the walls at work when I'm confronted with a puzzling situation. Nothing says, "Hey you, create a special interest group on software so programmers can exchange ideas and help one another solve problems."

I often know what I *should* do as a manager, but I rarely know what to do on the first day that I need to do it. Ideas usually come to me a day or week later. The time delay often makes a significant difference, affecting aspects that will contribute to the success or failure of a job or project, and so I find myself constantly in a struggle to cope with this time lapse. When no giant, yellow sign pops up at the time I need it, I feel that I've failed in some way as a manager.

Knowing that I have earned a small arsenal of professional certifications—some in the area of project management—can help me feel better about my professional worth, but one thing I have noticed is that there can be a big difference between what a person's certification indicates he should be capable of doing and his actual performance under pressure on the job. Certification usually requires that the candidate attend class, study materials, and take a fairly rigorous exam—but it doesn't always cover what one needs to master in order to face crossfire on the battlefield at work.

I obtained useful information while studying for my various certifications, some of which is easy to remember and apply on the job. Much of it, however, is stored like my management ideas. I eventually remember what I should do, but not on the day I really need to do it. Instead of looking for billboards to tell me what is coming, I have tried to train myself to notice other things, such as what I call my professional guerrillas, as well as ways to close gaps, and training.

GUERRILLAS

The problem I had that first day on the road crew was finding time to eat lunch. I wish my problems these days were so easy. More often, I struggle to convince the managers above me to try techniques that will improve our work. Early in my career as a manager, I usually failed at these attempts to convince. The upper managers had more faith in the status quo than in what I proposed we do instead. They had faith in the known instead of the unknown. In retrospect, I cannot blame them.

One day, I stumbled across some advice given by consultant and author Larry Constantine, which simply stated that people don't need permission to do a good job. That statement was liberating for me as I was always looking for permission from superiors. I suppose that behavior stemmed from my childhood and my belief in showing respect for elders. Those ideas were good when kept in the right context. My problem was that I was extending them to situations where they didn't apply. Constantine told of times during his career when he and his colleagues had tried to get permission to do a job differently, but couldn't get the permission they sought. Instead of continuing to use what they considered to be failing techniques, they gave themselves permission to do a good job; they empowered themselves to make the right decisions.

If I recall correctly, Constantine called this concept "guerrilla tactics at work," which I interpreted to mean: "If you know what to do but your managers won't let you do it, do it anyway. Do the right thing, regardless of policy. You may have to do it quietly, after hours, or by other surreptitious means, but do it."

I have met many managers who assume, as I did early in my career, that they can only do the things that someone above them has told them to do. They think they need permission to do what they feel is right. Some of you reading this may fall into another category, that of outgoing people who do what they think is best without pausing more than a second to consider what others may think. You may well have managers working for you who are not like you. They operate as I did, wanting to do good, but feeling they need permission first. You are probably wondering why these managers sit around doing nothing. Well, I believe they want your permission! Please give it to them. When they ask if they can do something, tell them Yes. In addition, tell them they always have permission to do what they think is good.

CLOSING THE GAP

As noted, I have sometimes seen a gap between a person's level of professional certification and level of performance. Sometimes, a manager has a formal certification with a title of project manager or team leader. The title is there, but the performance lags. What the person lacks is training.

Training

One way to close the gap between someone's knowledge of what to do and his or her being able to do it comes with training. Organizations spend large amounts of money to train their managers to manage their work. This is not a new method, but nothing in my experience has shown me that this approach really works. An organization that sends its project managers to training and assumes they then are qualified and able to implement that training may be in for a nasty surprise when the trained and qualified project managers make costly mistakes.

One form of training that works for me that I mentioned earlier in this book is experiential learning, whereby people experience a situation and then discuss how they felt and what they learned during the experience. Experiential learning differs from traditional training in several ways, most significantly with regard to the *source* of learning. In traditional training, the key is what the instructor teaches. In experiential learning, the key is what the student experiences. Because this learning originates inside the learner, it is far more likely to stay with the learner than does information coming from an outside source—as the expression goes, going in one ear and out the other. When a situation arises at work, the manager is more likely to remember the good thing to do.

I can remember some "lessons" that happened to me at the asphalt plant better than most of the lessons people actively have attempted to teach me. I well remember how hungry I was that day while putting up road signs. I also remember the satisfaction of finishing painting the black stripes and yellow stripes on the plant's safety rails. I vividly remember the feeling of frustration while standing in one spot all day flagging traffic. I remember these lessons because *I experienced them.* When I see someone who looks hungry, satisfied, or frustrated, I am better able to empathize with that person and do the right thing at the right time.

Experiential learning delves into what most managers in technical fields call that "touchy feely" emotional stuff. Most engineers and information technology professionals don't like emotional stuff. We prefer facts, figures, and machines. We deny that feelings play a part in doing real work. I have learned that we are wrong in our denials. I *do* have feelings while trying to manage work, and I am better able to recognize and deal with these feelings in myself and in others if I have learned about them by experiencing them.

BILLBOARDS ON MY DESK

Oh how I suffer because giant, yellow billboards don't pop up at work when I need them. To cope with what is missing, I create for myself some kind of clues and cues.

Writing helps me remember the good things I should do. Writing does not have the same effect on everyone. I have met people who wear a bracelet with special charms to remind them of something they know they should do. When they feel perplexed at work, they finger through their charms until they hit upon the right thing to do.

Another set of cues is a checklist. I carry a packet of three-inch by five-inch cards in my pocket on which to note items that pertain to the job I am currently doing. When I change jobs or projects, I change the card and note different items. When I feel powerless or confused (there are those feelings again), I pull a card from my pocket and read the cues. Sometimes, merely feeling a card in my fingers helps me to think more clearly and make better choices.

Notice the connection between feeling and thinking. I feel the card, I feel a boost in confidence, I am able to think more clearly. If I admit to myself that I, as an engineer and manager, have feelings, I can recognize and deal with those feelings. Then I am better able to think and make choices.

The card I carry in my pocket these days has the following questions written on it:

What would happen if . . . ?

What question will we ask after we answer that question?

How will we do that?

How will that help us reach our goal?

These questions are not specific to any context. I can use them whether I am trying to solve an engineering management problem or plan a family picnic. I also include questions to help me find the good thing I should do when no one will tell me to do it: *If I were a truly good manager, would what I be doing? What would be a good thing to do now?*

In most situations, I find answers to these and other questions. The problem that plagued me for years is that I didn't know what questions to ask myself. I finally realized that when I knew the question, I could find the answer. For a while, I tried to carry answers in my pocket, but there are too many different answers in life to fit in a shirt pocket. I carry the questions because there are only a few of them.

Thoughts on the Road Crew's Lunch Break

It's curious that I can recall what I did that first day on the road crew in 1977. I remember how anxious I was to make a good impression. At each new sign location, I jumped off the truck so I could grab a post-hole digger before anyone else. I attacked the ground with that digger to show the whole crew that I belonged out there with them. Such were the thoughts of an eighteen-year-old who wanted to impress others.

I also remember the anxiety I felt about lunch. I wondered silently to myself, *When are we ever going to stop and eat? When will the foreman tell me to take a break?* What I had too little job and life experience to ask was, "When will someone tell me to do something that any normal person would just do on his own?"

I have worked with many smart people in the years since that day. I include myself in that group. Often, we smart folks act like I did on that day. We know what we should be doing and we know that it is the right thing to do. Nevertheless, we stand around and do the wrong thing—either by omission or commission. *We want someone to tell us to do it or we want permission to do it.*

Conclusions

I learned so much while working at the asphalt plant. The men would occasionally pull me aside and talk to me about what was happening and explain the alternatives we had in the given situation. I treasured those moments, but what I treasure even more is the practice I had at the asphalt plant. We did things with our hands, our minds, and the machinery, again and again until practice made perfect (at least in some areas). *Doing* made an indelible impression on me. *Practicing* the many lessons I learned did more to prepare me for a career in engineering and management than any course I took while earning three engineering degrees. Among the practice-related experiences I had at the asphalt plant were these most memorable ones:

> *Time and practice are often both necessary.*
>
> *A little work, repeated, can accomplish much.*
>
> *Believing that theory equals reality can bring surprisingly unpleasant, bad results.*
>
> *Sometimes no one will tell you when to do something good for yourself.*

References

[KEI84]   D. Keirsey and M. Bates, *Please Understand Me: Character and Temperament Types*, 4th ed. (Del Mar, Calif.: Prometheus Nemesis Book Co., 1984).

[MYE80]   I.B. Myers, *Gifts Differing* (Palo Alto, Calif.: Consulting Psychologists Press, 1980).

[OBR04]   R. O'Bryan and D. Phillips, *It Sounded Good When We Started: A Project Manager's Guide to Working With People on Projects* (New York: IEEE Computer Society Press/John Wiley and Sons, 2004).

[PHI04]   D. Phillips, *The Software Project Manager's Handbook: Principles That Work at Work*, 2nd ed. (New York: IEEE Computer Society, 2004).

[WEI86]   G.M. Weinberg, *Becoming a Technical Leader: A Problem-Solving Approach* (New York: Dorset House Publishing, 1986).

[WEI94]   ——, *Quality Software Management, Vol. 3: Congruent Action* (New York: Dorset House Publishing, 1994).

[WEI97]   ——, *Quality Software Management, Vol. 4: Anticipating Change* (New York: Dorset House Publishing, 1997).

Hiring the Best Knowledge Workers, Techies & Nerds

The Secrets & Science of Hiring Technical People

by Johanna Rothman
foreword by Gerald M. Weinberg

ISBN: 978-0-932633-59-0
©2004 352 pages softcover
$43.95 (includes $6 UPS in US)

*Proven Methods for Attracting,
Interviewing, and Hiring Technical Workers*

Good technical people are the foundation on which successful high technology organizations are built. Establishing a good process for hiring such workers is essential. Unfortunately, the generic methods so often used for hiring skill-based staff, who can apply standardized methods to almost any situation, are of little use to those charged with the task of hiring technical people.

Hiring the Best takes the guess-work out of hiring and diminishes the risk of costly hiring mistakes. With the aid of step-by-step descriptions and detailed examples, you'll learn how to • write a concise, targeted job description • source candidates • develop ads for mixed media • review résumés quickly to determine Yes, No, or Maybe candidates • develop intelligent, nondiscriminatory, interview techniques • create fool-proof phone-screens • check references with a view to reading between the lines • extend an offer that will attract a win-win acceptance or tender a gentle-but-decisive rejection • and more.

Read more about HIRING THE BEST *at www.dorsethouse.com/books/hire.html*

"It's not enough to hire 'good enough' . . . you need to hire the best, and nobody knows more than Johanna Rothman about that. This clear and comprehensive book joins *Peopleware* and *The Mythical Man Month* as must-reads for technical managers."

—Joel Spolsky, Founder, Fog Creek Software

"Rothman lays out the tasks and the issues, then addresses actual situations that might arise. She covers the entire subject thoroughly. . . .

"If you are a hiring manager in a high-tech field, you must read this book."

—Richard Mateosian, IEEE Micro

Weinberg on Writing
The Fieldstone Method

by Gerald M. Weinberg

ISBN: 978-0-932633-65-1   ©2006
208 pages   softcover
$30.95 (includes $6 UPS in US)

The Writing Method That Works for One of Our Most Prolific and Popular Authors

Gerald M. Weinberg, author of more than forty books—including eighteen published by Dorset House—reveals his secrets for collecting and organizing his ideas for writing projects.

Drawing an analogy to the stone-by-stone method of building fieldstone walls, Weinberg shows writers how to construct fiction and nonfiction manuscripts from key insights, stories, and quotes. The elements, or stones, are collected nonsequentially, over time, and eventually find logical places in larger pieces.

The method renders writer's block irrelevant and has proved effective for scores of Weinberg's writing class students. If you've ever wanted to write a book or article—or need to revitalize your writing career—don't miss this intimate glimpse into the mind behind some the computer industry's best books.

If you've ever wanted to write a book or article—or need to revitalize your writing career -- don't miss this intimate glimpse into the mind behind some the computer industry's best books.

Read more about WEINBERG ON WRITING *at www.dorsethouse.com/books/wow.html*

"Don't write your book—build it with Weinberg's Fieldstone Method. Keep the project moving by breaking the project into easy-to-attack chunks; gather your ideas one at a time. Then stack them as you would stones in a wall."
—**Dan Poynter**, author of
Writing Nonfiction and *The Self-Publishing Manual*

". . . this book on 'constructing' writing, so to speak, is a delight. . . . In demystifying the mysterious process of writing through the consistent metaphoric grappling hook of 'fieldstones' as ideas which float in and out of our consciousness, Weinberg has written a wise and warm book on overcoming the perils of trying to write."
—**Gabriele Rico**, author of
Writing the Natural Way